KING OF HEAVEN, LORD OF EARTH

To

Gary + Raiza, & Family

With my thanks &
very best wishes in the
Lord Jesus,

Steve Brady

20th May '06.

Col 1 15-20

KING OF HEAVEN
LORD OF EARTH

A Study Guide for the Letter to the Colossians

Steve Brady
and Elizabeth McQuoid

First published 2003 by Keswick Ministries and Authentic Lifestyle

09 08 07 06 05 04 03   7 6 5 4 3 2 1

Reprinted 2004 by Authentic Media
9 Holdom Avenue, Bletchley, Milton Keynes, MK1 1QR, UK
and PO Box 1047, Waynesboro, GA 30830-2047, USA
www.authenticmedia.co.uk

British Library Cataloguing in Publication Data

A catalogue record for this book is available from the British Library

1-85078-848-1

Cover design by
Sam Redwood
Print Management by Adare Carwin
Printed and bound by AIT Nørhaven A/S, Denmark

This is a book that unwraps the message of Colossians and places it slap bang in the middle of our 21st century world. Whether you read it alone or as part of a group, you will discover what makes Jesus Christ so special.

Ian Coffey, Senior Minister, Mutley Baptist Church, Plymouth

Few people are as able to communicate theological truth in a way that 'grounds' it into our everyday life, as Steve Brady. If you want to know what it means for 'God's will in heaven to be done on earth' then this book is for you. I enthusiastically commend it.

John Glass, General Superintendent, Elim

This study guide does not shirk the difficult bits of Colossians; it is under-girded by solid learning and sound theology. But it wears its learning with such modesty and handles the big topics with such lightness of touch that you are stimulated to think and pray creatively rather than weighted down by theory. Which is, of course, what a letter from Paul was designed to do! Get it for your house/cell group leaders, preaching team – and yourself.

Rt Rev Jonathan Gledhill, Bishop of Southampton

Colossians, with its emphasis on the glory and sufficiency of Christ, is one of the most necessary letters for Christians today to get to grips with. And with contemporary illustrations and non-technical language this volume brings alive, especially for small groups, Paul's glorious theme.

Andy Paterson, President FIEC,
Senior Pastor of Kensington Baptist Church, Bristol

Biblical, lively, practical, creative… a terrific resource for everyone wanting to get to grips with Paul's message to the Colossians.

Alistair Begg, Parkside Church, USA

Here is a book that is sound, solid but also beautifully simple – an exceedingly rare combination. It is Steve at his best interpreting Paul the Apostle at his best – Colossians.

R T Kendall

Only a true scholar could make the text so accessible, only a gifted preacher could present it with such relevance, and only one with a true pastor's heart could apply it so warmly. Steve Brady is uniquely blessed in being all three.

Rev Robert Amess, Chairman of the Evangelical Alliance

Colossians is opened up, served up and warmed up by this highly readable study-guide. Warm style, discerning digging, relevant illustration and altogether a teaching guide accessible to everyone.

Rt Rev Michael Baughen

The book of Colossians has much to say to today's society with its New Age philosophy and multi-cultural context. This study guide encourages us to face up to what God's word is saying and the poignant questions at the end of each section really make you stop and think!

Rev Dr Rob Frost

In a masterly exegesis of Colossians, Steve opens up the Word to show how amazingly relevant Paul's message of 2000 years ago is for us in the 21st century. Let's study well and apply thoroughly!

Peter Maiden, Chairman of the Keswick Convention

Contents

THE AIM OF THIS STUDY GUIDE

The aim of this study guide is to help bridge the gap between the Bible world and our own. Steve Brady's commentary digs deep into the letter to the Colossians and opens up the world of these first century believers to us. The questions that follow help relate the principles he draws out to our own lives and situations. You can use this guide either for your own devotional time with God or as part of a group. Enjoy your study!

USING THIS BOOK FOR PERSONAL STUDY

Begin by praying and reading through the passage and commentary a number of times before looking at the questions.

You may find it helpful to note down your answers to the questions and any other thoughts you may have. Putting pen to paper will help you think through the issues and how they specifically apply to your own situation. It will also be encouraging to look back over all that God has been teaching you!

Talk about what you are learning with a friend. Pray together that you will be able to apply all these new lessons to your life.

USING THIS BOOK IN SMALL GROUPS

You will probably only have time to cover one chapter of the study guide per session. However, the guide is designed so that you can decide which chapters you want to use in the sessions you have available. Each passage of Scripture is explored over three chapters of the study guide, looking at key verses each week. Read the passage of Scripture, decide what key verses your group should spend time looking at and then direct them to the corresponding chapters of the study guide.

In preparation for the study, pray and read the passage of Scripture and commentary over a number of times. Use other resource material such as a Bible dictionary or atlas if they would be helpful.

Each week think through what materials you need for the study – a flip chart, pens and paper, other Bible translations, worship tapes – and read the chapter carefully.

At the top of each chapter we have stated the aim – this is the heart of the passage and the truth you want your group to take away with them. With this in mind, decide which questions and activities you should spend most time on. Add questions that would be helpful to your particular group or church situation.

Before people come, encourage them to read the passage and commentary that you will be studying each week.

Make sure you leave time at the end of the study for people to 'Reflect and Respond' so they are able to apply what they are learning to their own situations.

Introduction

Do you remember the song Bob Dylan sang years ago, *The times they are a-changing?* His sentiments certainly ring true today. In my native Liverpool, I remember that people seemed at least to be honest and decent and, growing up in the fifties, you could always leave your door open. Do you remember those days? We used to joke that if someone had broken in and had a look around, they would leave a pound on the mantelpiece for my mum – it was that kind of place! Today security is tight: everything has to be tacked down and locked up. The times they are a-changing.

People look at the world differently now. We are constantly being told that we are moving from a period of modernity to post-modernity. That is a slippery term to define, to be sure, but the results are plain to see. At life's genesis we tolerate nearly two hundred thousand abortions a year in the UK; at life's exodus there is a growing call for euthanasia, mercy killing. We have a rampant crime rate, and huge problems with drug and alcohol abuse. And did you know that the porn industry has a larger dollar turn-over in the USA than tobacco, alcohol and drugs combined? Here in the UK, we have one of the highest rates of divorce in the world. And what is so sad for the thoughtful Christian is that we are seeing many of these problems surfacing in the church. Statistically, the church seems to be little better than the world in which she is placed. We seem to be living in a moral and spiritual vacuum. Because both nature and grace abhor vacuums, all sorts of alternative spiritualities have been sucked into that vacuum that the Christian gospel used to fill. People pick and mix their beliefs, and truth is what is true for me — at least what I feel to be true today — tomorrow I may feel differently.

Paul also lived in a world that was riddled with both polytheism, the belief in many gods, and pluralism — there are many ways to God and many ways to behave and live. The early Christians faced many of the same kind of problems that we are facing today. When we turn to the church at Colosse, the key probably appears to be what we would call syncretism. Syncretism says, you can have Jesus, but also, alongside Jesus, you can have a few other spiritual masters (and mistresses!) too. It is like buying a car that isn't top of the range. The salesman tempts you to add a satellite navigation system, alloys, cruise control and air conditioning. You add to your basic model as you go along. You take some things, leave others and plan to come back another time for the rest. Similarly, the question for the Colossian church was 'Is Jesus Christ sufficient in a world full of myth and magic?' Or did they need to supplement their faith by going to other powers and authorities? If someone was sick, should her friends pray over her in the name of Jesus, but also go to the local shaman or witch-doctor equivalent for help as well, ensuring that some incantation was intoned over the friend, just in case Jesus didn't show up?

In Colosse, Jesus was eminent. He had status. The real question was 'Is he pre-eminent?' Jesus was important, just not all-important; adequate but not totally sufficient for every need. In this last century, Mahatma Gandhi said: 'I cannot ascribe exclusive divinity to Jesus. He is as divine as Krishna or Rama or Mohammed or Zoroaster.' Jesus is then a *comparative*. He *compares* well with others. That was the kind of problem here in Colosse. He was a comparative, not a *superlative*. He was better, not the best. He was penultimate but not ultimate. He was more but not all.

So this is why Paul writes to these Colossian Christians. He is warning them of the real danger involved in turning to another Jesus who is less than the Jesus of the Bible, the Son of the living God. If they failed to heed his warning, their faith and everything associated with it would eventually unravel. Their trade-in of the real Jesus would give them a domesticated Jesus, a Jesus who may be Lord of some things but not Lord of all. That is why Colossians is so important for the church today, a church in a world full of pluralistic ideologies, philosophies and religions all competing for our attention and devotion. Colosse was a church that had to find its way in the world of its day, without the advantage of all the background knowledge Christians have today, after centuries of Christian civilisation. Yet Colosse was part of a first century missionary church that outlived, out-thought and out-died its contemporary world and passed on the baton of faith. This letter, if we will listen to it, will provide challenge, inspiration and a renewed focus to keep on living for Christ in our generation. Be encouraged as you study this epistle to the Colossians. In it, we discover the resources we need to live for Jesus in our world and its changing religious and spiritual challenges.

Chapter 1 – Identity

Aim: To discover our Christian identity

Focus on the theme

At the beginning of this study, introduce yourselves. Take time to go round the group asking each person to describe themselves, who they see themselves as being. Take notice of how people identify themselves.

Read: Colossians 1:1-14
Key verses: Colossians 1:1-2

At one level, when Paul wrote his letters, he wrote like anybody else in the first century. He used the typical formula for epistles – he would start with thanksgiving. Then he would move into the content of what he wished to communicate – the substance of the letter. Finally, there would be a few concluding remarks, and maybe a signature at the end.

He introduced himself as 'Paul an apostle' (v1). Now the word apostle in Scripture literally means 'sent one'. The Latin equivalent is missionary. At one level, every Christian is a sent one; we have been sent by the risen Christ into the world. But there is an exclusive sense to this word too. When Paul says he is an apostle, he means he is someone who has seen the risen Lord and has been personally commissioned by him as a bearer of the apostolic gospel (see I Cor. 9:1-2; 15:1-8). So verse 5 mentions the 'word of truth', and verse 6 knowing 'God's grace in all its truth.' He is an apostle, not as a result of deciding to get a new day job because he thought that Judaism had had its day. Rather, it was the will of God (v1). He had been converted on the Damascus road, he had seen the risen Lord and had been commissioned by him.

 • *What difference does it make to your life to know that you are a sent one?*

What is your prison?

If it was the will of God for Paul to be an apostle, it was also God's will for him to write this letter. Colossians is one of Paul's prison epistles, written around the same time as Ephesians, Philippians and Philemon. Paul found a writing ministry when he was in prison for the gospel. I don't suppose he would have willingly signed up for that, but he realised it was the will of God that he should be in prison at that time. Whilst there, he had the time to think and write to these various churches. In prison by the will of God? That is a jarring note for many Christians today. To be a success, to be a winner, to be always on the up, surely that is the will of God? Isn't it God's will for me always to be healthy, wealthy and wise, so I can 'name it, claim it and then frame it'? Or, if it goes wrong, blame it on someone or something! But here Paul is in prison by the will of God.

Are you in circumstances you would not choose for yourself? What is your prison? Is it illness, heartbreak, redundancy, bereavement, the onset of old age? Whatever your prison is, God can use it for his purposes, just as he did for Paul. From prison Paul was able to write this letter that has blessed count-less generations of believers. God can use your prison for his glory too – Romans 8:28.

 • *Does it help you deal with your particular hardship knowing that it is there by the will of God? Explain your answer.*

In Colosse, in Christ

Paul is writing to 'the holy and faithful brothers in Christ' (v2). Originally these were terms reserved for the Jews. But in this church at Colosse there are now Jews and Gentiles. People with diverse backgrounds and experiences are now accepted as the people of God. They are the holy and faithful brothers.

Paul goes on to address them as 'in Christ at Colosse.' What Paul literally wrote was 'in Colosse, in Christ', not 'at Colosse'. The Christian has a dual address. We live both in Christ and in Colosse. When we forget either of those addresses we are in big trouble.

Paul is writing to the church in Colosse, a fairly insignificant place at the time, situated in the Lycus Valley, now part of modern Turkey. This church faced different circumstances and challenges to the churches at Hieropolis and Laodicea, both just a few miles up the road. It had seen better days, like some of the towns and cities we individually come from.

Beware when people have got a one-size-fits-all solution to your church problem. Churches are different! Do you know where you live? I don't just mean your address. Do you know the kind of place you come from, the kind of people your church is seeking to serve? There is a great danger, when we don't know where we live, that we become a Christian ghetto. We are not part of the community we serve, we don't incarnate. Instead, we just drive into church, bolt ourselves in and then drive off again. We need to learn to live where God has placed us, because where God has placed us has a bearing on how we maintain our witness to the gospel in that community.

● *This letter could have been addressed to us – 'to the holy and faithful brothers in Christ at …' How can we be called holy? In what sense are we already holy and in what sense are we becoming holy? Explain your answer.*

● *On a flip chart, brainstorm together the features of your local community. Who are the people you are trying to reach with the gospel?*

● *Are there better ways of reaching the people in your community with the gospel? What other events or methods could you try and what events should you cancel?*

However, where you come from isn't all that important. It is being in Christ that makes all the difference. That is why Paul can later say, despite the diversity of our backgrounds, there is 'no Greek or Jew, circumcised or uncircumcised, barbarian, Scythian, slave or free, but Christ is all, and is in all!' (Col. 3:11). Being a Christian is being in Christ. This is one of Paul's regularly repeated phrases; he uses it dozens of times. What gives me my identity isn't just where I live or where I come from; rather it is whose I am, and to whom I belong. I am in Christ and I am in my Colosse. It isn't either/or. If I am just in my Colosse, I will capitulate to my culture. If I am just in Christ, I may not be able to relate to my culture.

● *Look up other references for 'in Christ' (for example 1:4,28; 2:9-10,17). Try and come up with a group definition for what this means.*

So believers are in Christ and in Colosse. This is how Christian identity is formed. Christian identity is made up of where you have come from and where you are going. And where you are going is far more important than where you have come from! What gives me my identity – my genes, my family background, my community, my education, my job? Obviously all these factors have a bearing. But what is crucial is being in Christ. I am no longer simply the person I was, defined by my Colosse, all explicable on the horizontal plane. I am in Christ, a new person, with a changed destiny because, on the vertical plane,

Christ has stepped into my life. In him I have resources I did not have before. For instance, I have 'grace and peace from God our Father' (v2). The resources I need to live the Christian life do not come through merely human agencies. God our Father supplies what we need to live the life he has designed us for.

- *Grace and peace are familiar Christian terms but how would you explain them to a non-Christian?*

- *What practical tips can you think of to remember your true Christian identity when things get tough this week?*

Reflection and response

Go round the room and introduce yourselves again. Explain to people where your Colosse is. Remember your dual identity! In twos, discuss what is happening in your Colosse in the coming week. Pray for each other. Perhaps ring one person up from your group during the week to encourage them to live in Christ, in Colosse.

Chapter 2 – Stability

Aim: To discover the key to stability in our Christian lives

Focus on the theme

We all have ups and downs in our spiritual lives. When you are down, what practices, events, people or places help you get back on track?

Read: Colossians 1:1-14
Key verses: Colossians 1:3-8

Gospel people

Paul continues, 'We always thank God, the Father of our Lord Jesus Christ, when we pray for you' (v3). That is a very apostolic note. He often begins his letters by saying this sort of thing (Galatians is an exception!) When he is planning to talk to these Christians, he knows there are things he needs to say, some of which will be painful. But he is not just interested in telling it as it is. He knows these Christians need encouragement, so he tells them why he is grateful to God for them. He thanks God for their faith in Christ, their personal trust and commitment to him as Lord and Saviour. What makes this church a church is this: they are gospel people. They believe the gospel. Denominational labels are not nearly as important as whether the church you are a part of is a gospel church that proclaims

life and freedom and forgiveness of sins in and through Jesus
Christ.

● *What part does/should encouragement from other Christians
   play in keeping us stable and on track in our faith?*

● *What do we learn from Paul's example about how to encourage
   people and what to encourage them for?*

Love for one another

Next, he mentions their love for the saints (v4). How do you
know somebody is a Christian? Because they made a profession
of faith by walking down an aisle in response to an invitation,
although they never want to be anywhere near the people they
are going to spend eternity with? I don't think so. Faith in Jesus
Christ produces a love for the people of God, fellow Christians,
that comes from the Holy Spirit (see v8). It is a new affection
for a group of people with whom, at one time, you would not
have been seen dead – the church! Church is meant to be the
privilege of the redeemed, not the punishment you have to
undergo in some sort of Protestant purgatory before you go
to heaven. As Jesus said, 'By this shall all men know that you are
my disciples, that you have love for one another' (Jn. 13:35).

Notice that this is love for all the saints, not just people
whom you personally like. Churches are not supposed to be
monochrome, designer churches, full of like-minded people. It
is easy to love people just like yourself, isn't it? But what real
faith produces is a love for all the saints. God's purpose through
the gospel is to produce a new community from a damaged
humanity and a loving society out of a hateful world. It is
shocking if we think that love in the church is some kind of
optional extra. As the saying goes: 'people don't care how much
you know; they want to know how much you care.' If your

church is a bit low on the love stakes, then your church is in big, big trouble.

> To me, t'was not the truth you taught,
> To you so clear, to me still dim,
> But when you came you brought
> A sense of him.
>
> Not merely in the words you say,
> Not only in your deeds confessed,
> But in the most unconscious way
> Is Christ expressed
>
> Is it a beatific smile
> A holy light up in your brow?
> Oh no! I felt His presence
> When you laughed just now.
>
>
> And from your eyes He beckons me,
> And from your heart His love is shed.
> Till I lose sight of you and see
> The Christ instead.

- *What kind of criteria are we tempted to use to judge whether someone is a Christian?*

- *In this passage, what criteria does Paul use to decide if someone is a Christian? What are the key differences in your two lists?*

Hope

Such faith and love spring from hope. Literally, Paul says 'the faith and love that spring from the hope that is stored up for you in heaven' (v5). How can you keep going on with Christ year in and year out, beset with problems and perhaps a less than perfect church? What keeps you fired up? Paul says it is hope stored up in heaven. There are all sorts of side-benefits that come into your life when you become a Christian. You get a sense of purpose, joy, peace, and happiness. But you can get a lot of these feelings by just taking drugs. If God just wanted us to be happy, he would have simply sent us Prozac! But he does not just want us to be happy; he wants us to be holy. He does not want us just satisfied; he wants us sanctified, made like Christ. And there's something important we need to remember. Whatever benefits we receive from the gospel now – and they are considerable – are only foretastes. The big deal, the big payload of the gospel, will not come until we see Jesus – it is stored up for you in heaven. The best is yet to come! Whatever we have received already, you ain't seen nothing yet! Don't fall for the lie that you can have it all now. You will have it all in heaven. One of the secrets of living the Christian life in a God-honouring way is to work out what is for the here and now and what is for the then and there.

- *Share practical examples of how the hope of heaven has shaped your decisions, values and priorities.*

- *How does the hope of heaven give stability to our Christian lives?*

The growing gospel

Verse 6 reminds us that 'All over the world this gospel is bearing fruit and growing.' There is an echo here of the 'Be fruitful and multiply' theme that harks back to the book of Genesis. Back then, mankind disobeyed and brought both a curse and

chaos into God's world. Now, through the gospel, God is reversing that curse which one day will mean there will be a new
heaven and a new earth. Paul is confident that the gospel of
Christ is growing and increasing. How?

Firstly, it is via hearing the 'word of truth' (v5). Evangelism
entails verbal proclamation, words. We live in an image-conscious
age, with brand names and jealously guarded logos. If Christians,
however, only use symbols – a cross or a fish for instance – and
don't explain them, the gospel isn't heard. And then it isn't
'understood' (v6). The gospel is something we need to hear.
Verse 7 adds that the gospel is something we therefore learn.
The Colossians learned it from Epaphras. In our culture in the
UK today, post Christian many say, we need to give people the
opportunity to learn the gospel – *Alpha, Christianity Explored,*
the *Y Course* etc.

I learned the gospel from a man called Ron Shaw, my YPF
leader. One night, that YPF leader took a group of us to hear the
gospel from a man called Ken Terhoven, who put the fear of God
into me. I was not saved that night in January 1967, but I was in
deep turmoil and conviction of sin. I learned the gospel from him.
A few weeks later, on 13 March 1967 at about 9:15pm to be pre-
cise(!), I learned the gospel from a man called Malcolm Smith who
preached Christ and pointed the way to Jesus and his cross. I was
converted that night. I further learned the gospel from a great Bible
teacher, my old pastor, Richard Darnell. He taught me the word of
God. And then I learned the gospel from Gilbert Kirby, the
Principal, and a whole host of faithful teachers at London Bible
College, where I trained for full-time ministry. Praise God for men
and women like Epaphras who faithfully teach the word of God.

- *How has people's understanding of these key words changed in
  the past fifty to a hundred years?*

  - *Truth*
  - *Gospel*

- *God*
- *Church*
- *Christian*

- *Christian stability depends on having good foundations and learning the gospel. Given that people's understanding of Christian things has changed so much over the years, how can we help them learn the gospel? What do we need to be doing as a church and as individuals?*

- *Sum up all you think this passage says about how we can have stability in our Christian lives. How will this help you cope differently in future with life's spiritual ups and downs?*

Further study

- *Look up Romans 5:2-5, Galatians 5:5-6, 1 Thessalonians 1:3, 5:8, and compare Hebrews 10:22-24 to learn more about Paul's favourite trio of faith, hope and love.*
- *Find out more about our hope of heaven in 1 Peter 1:4, 2 Timothy 4:8 and Revelation 21:1-8.*

Reflection and response

On one side of a piece of paper, write down all the people who have been like Epaphras to you, all the people who have taught you the gospel. On the other side, write down the people God has placed in your life to whom you can be an Epaphras. Spend time thanking God for the people who have taught you the gospel and invested so much in you! Then in twos, pray for each other that God would help you be an Epaphras to someone else, and that your lives would be marked by the stability that knowing Christ brings.

Chapter 3 – Maturity

Aim: To grow in Christian maturity

Focus on the theme

If you had a spiritual gauge somewhere on your body, how would it read? Brainstorm together what criteria we use to check our spiritual health and growth towards maturity.

Read: Colossians 1:1–14
Key verses: Colossians 1:9–14

God's rescue plan

In verses 12-14 Paul, who has echoed the Book of Genesis in verse 6, now piles on terms that were associated with the motley Israelite crew that came out of Egypt at the Exodus. Here we have phrases that are loaded with Old Testament allusions. Paul reminds the Colossians that they had been rescued from the 'dominion of darkness' (v13) – darkness being one of the great plagues of Egypt. God has brought us into the kingdom, 'the kingdom of the Son, in whom we have redemption, the forgiveness of sins' (v14). These Old Testament phrases are now being used to describe what happens when someone becomes a Christian. A great transfer has occurred, a great rescue has taken place. God rescues us from 'the dominion of darkness', that is the authority, the power of darkness. If I am not a Christian, according to Scripture, I am under the power and sway of darkness.

People in the grip of darkness sometimes illustrate that bondage by incredibly cruel lifestyles, or outlandish sins of the flesh. Primarily, however, the grip of darkness itself is a heart of rebellion that thinks: I don't need Christ; I can do it my way; I can be independent of God. Under the power of darkness, we can do nothing to save ourselves. Thank God, the gospel isn't a 'pull yourself up by your own bootstraps' message. Our danger is so great, our plight so terrible, it is only God Almighty who can mount the rescue mission. The gospel is our God coming personally in Christ to rescue us from the dominion of sin. That rescue, effected through the cross, brings us redemption (v14). It buys us out of slavery. It sets us free. It brings us forgiveness.

C.S. Lewis, the well-known Oxford don and later Cambridge professor, was once on an *Any Questions* type programme. He was asked, ' Professor Lewis, what can Jesus Christ give me that no one else can give me, and I want the answer in just one word?' And without hesitating a moment, that great Christian scholar simply said, 'Forgiveness.' The gospel offers us forgiveness. I don't have to work off my bad karma, or atone for my sins. In trusting to Jesus Christ, I am set free from the grip of darkness because I come under the rule and management of a new authority, the kingdom of Jesus (v13).

- *On a big sheet of A4 or a flipchart, list the phrases Paul uses to describe God's rescue plan in verses 12-14.*

- *These phrases are loaded with Old Testament imagery. What images could you use to describe God's rescue plan to a modern reader?*

- *What do verses 12-14 say to people who reject God, thinking that they are independent, free agents?*
- *Why is forgiveness such a priceless commodity? Think about the forgiveness between us and God and ourselves and other people.*

How does this transfer from the kingdom of darkness into the kingdom of light come about? Verse 12 tells us. God has qualified us. I remember when I was one of the guinea pigs on a new degree course, many years ago. I had to sit a Hebrew exam that nobody had tried before. I sat there for three hours, most of the time just praying! It might as well have been Sanskrit. I came out, my head whizzing – I was sure I had failed. But everyone else had the same problem. The exam had been set at a standard that only Regius Professors of Hebrew at Oxford and Cambridge could cope with. So the examiners got together and they must have decided that my name on the paper alone was worth at least 30%! They qualified the whole lot of us. We all passed. It was a miracle. Sheer grace. It bore no relationship to my per-formance or deserts. Likewise, God qualifies us by his grace. To put it another way, Christ has taken the exam for us, but inserts our name, not his – and we therefore pass because of his efforts not ours.

● *God's rescue plan demonstrates sheer grace to us that we should demonstrate to others. Share together examples of when someone in the Body of Christ has shown you grace.*

● *How can we make grace more of a feature of our lives?*

Go the distance

This great transfer was just the start of the Christian life for these Colossians. Paul wants them to press on towards maturity. He prays for God 'to fill you with the knowledge of his will through all spiritual wisdom and understanding' (v9). The purpose? 'That you may live a life worthy of the Lord and may please him in every way: bearing fruit in every good work... being strengthened with all power according to his glorious might' (v10, 11). Are we to be happy, peaceful and contented? Not in the first instance. Rather, that we may have 'great endurance and patience' (v11). Are we then stoical, tight-lipped, determined and miserable? Hardly. Note the addition, 'joyfully'! Paul prays that these Christians will go the distance of faith. To do that, they need to be helped to see the big game plan, the big picture. Without such spiritual insight, they will lose their way. They will live merely for the here and now. Paul prays that they will remember that, from eternity to eternity, God's rescue plan is in Christ. Since it is from here to eternity, he prays that they might have 20:20 spiritual vision to grasp and hold on to the purposes of God in Christ.

Like these Colossians, we too need spiritual insight, sticka-bility and endurance to tough it out 'with joy' – the literal translation of verse 11. This is joy inspired by the Holy Spirit, the kind that gives us strength – see Nehemiah 8:10. In this way, we will be able to 'live a life worthy of the Lord and please him in every way' (v10).

You may know the film *Saving Private Ryan*. It recounts a story from the Second World War, post D-Day, when incredible American resources are used to rescue one soldier, Private Ryan, since all his brothers have already been killed in action. Many men lose their lives to save this one man. In a moving scene, towards the end of the film, the dying Captain of the rescue platoon, played by Tom Hanks, says to Ryan, 'Earn this! Earn what has been done for you.' In the final scene of the film, we see Private Ryan as an old man. He is visiting the graves of some of those who had given their lives for him and he is asking himself this pointed ques-tion: 'Was I good enough? Was I good enough, for all that has been done for me?' The cross of Jesus Christ says Christ has earned it. We were never good enough. He did it for us. But out of sheer gratitude to him, we are called to lay our lives down for him, daily and consistently following Jesus because 'love so amazing, so divine, demands my soul, my life, my all.' That is what is entailed in pleasing him 'in every way' and 'every good work' (v10).

- *Verse 11 says that part of maturity is being able to combine endurance with joy. Has this been possible in your own experience?*

- *In twos, look at all the characteristics of Christian maturity in verses 9-13. Come up with practices to put in place in your life that will encourage spiritual maturity. As a group, agree on your top five tips for maturity that will encourage one another to press on.*

Further study

- *What is spiritual wisdom? Look at the uses of the word 'wisdom' in Colossians 1:9, 28, 2:4. Also look at Proverbs 2.*
- *What does it mean to know God's will? To help your investigation, use a concordance to look for the other times Paul uses the phrase 'God's will.'*

Reflection and response

Worship God for his plan of salvation. Use the list you made in question 1 to aid your prayers. Make sure every one can see the flip chart or sheet of paper. Perhaps you could listen to a CD or sing some worship songs together.

Then individually list on a piece of paper the things you do in an average day; dropping the children off at school, seeing clients, travelling on the train etc. In all of these things, how could you live a life worthy of the Lord and please him in every way? Decide to tackle one of these areas this week. Remember to ask each other next week how you got on.

Review of Colossians 1:1-14

Read through Paul's prayer again. What have you learnt from his example about how to pray more biblically for the members of your small group and wider church? What ideas would Paul's prayer give you for praying for:

- *A young Christian mother at home with her three children*
- *A Christian businessman who has to travel away from home a lot*
- *A Christian teacher facing an OFSTED inspection next week*
- *A teenager going away to University for the first time*

Points to Ponder

- *What have you learnt about God?*
- *What have you learnt about yourself?*
- *What actions or attitudes do you need to change as a result?*

Chapter 4 – Christ's authority

Aim: To depend on Christ's authority because he is king of creation

Focus on the theme

Imagine yourself being cast away on a desert island. What three things would you take? You can only take one book, one piece of music and one luxury item! This is intended to be a fun exercise but also to provoke our thinking about what we ultimately need for survival.

Read: Colossians 1:15-29
Key verses: Colossians 1:15-17

The image of the invisible God

Some commentators suggest that verses 15-20 were originally a Christian hymn, written either by Paul or an anonymous hymn-writer in the early church. Either way, Paul decided to weave it into this letter to the Colossians. Scholars continue to debate this possibility, but what is obvious is the sheer richness of this passage. Paul tells us firstly that Jesus is the image of the invisible God (v15). We live in an image-conscious age. Image is everything. What is important is what you project, not who you really are. In fact, the words 'spin' and 'spin doctoring' have become very popular. It isn't the reality that counts; it is how you spin the thing.

Confucianism teaches that there are three important elements to a person. There is the person you think you are; there is the person others think you are; finally there is the person you really are. Image and reality are not the same. The further what you are is from what you project, the more likely you are to have psychological problems, since so much energy is being spent on projecting and protecting an image which is a façade. We are then like an actor playing a role, projecting an image, hiding behind a mask. Now is that what Paul means when he says Jesus is the image of the invisible God? Is he a projection of God, but not the reality? Does he give you an idea of what God is like but not the real thing? That isn't what Paul means to convey at all. Rather, the idea of image here is one of exactness, of representation, of revelation, of manifestation.

In the ancient world, if you made an image of yourself, it was viewed as part of you, as almost you. Paul is saying that Jesus is the image of the invisible God. He isn't different from God. He is the exact representation of God; he is the exact image. Hebrews chapter 1 will talk about the Son as the perfect image of God, the exact representation of his being. So, what God is you see in the Son. We sometimes say: 'like father, like son.' But Scripture wants us to see like Son, like Father. That is the picture. What the Father is, so is the Son. Therefore, in Jesus I don't meet someone who can introduce me to the ultimate God; in Jesus I meet God with a human face. I meet God in our shape and size.

John 1:18 puts it like this: 'No one has ever seen God, but God the One and Only, who is at the Father's side, has made him known.' 'Made known' is literally 'exegeted'! In biblical studies, exegesis is the art of explaining, drawing out, revealing what a passage says. Its opposite is eisegesis – putting into Scripture what isn't there. Jesus has 'exegeted' God, has revealed and explained him. Do you want to know what God is like? He is just like Jesus.

- *In Jesus we meet God with a human face. Brainstorm all the things we learn about God from the character of Jesus. Write your answers on a flipchart.*

- *Many people don't like reading the Old Testament because they believe they only see a God of wrath. They prefer the New Testament because they find there a loving Jesus. If Jesus truly is the image of God, how does that help us respond to this wrong way of thinking?*

- *It is often easier for us to grasp that Jesus was God rather than that he was fully human. What did it mean for Jesus to be truly human? Look up Hebrews 2:14-18, 4:15, and 5:7-8 for some ideas.*

Jesus the firstborn

Paul goes on to talk about Jesus as the firstborn (v15). Taken out of its context, 'the firstborn over all creation' has led some folk to deduce that Jesus is a created being. They think God's first creative act was to make the person we know now as Jesus. But that would be a massive mistake. The Bible does not say 'first created over all creation.' No, the word is 'firstborn', and it is loaded with Old Testament history. For instance, it was a word used of the ancient people of God. In Exodus 4:22 Israel was called God's firstborn, though it certainly was not the first created nation. And then the Davidic king, the one who was going to come, is called the firstborn in Psalm 89:27. What does it mean to be firstborn? It is to do with rank and status. It is to do with priority. It was a word that had increasingly little to do with birth at all, but rather the idea of being an heir. The Greeks had at least two words for 'first created' – if Paul had wanted to say Jesus was the first created being, he could have easily used one of them. But he says he is the firstborn. Just as the Uncreated Father stands before, above and beyond all his creation, so the Uncreated Son stands in that same position. He is the eternal Son of God.

These ideas run counter to much present thinking. The fact that creation itself isn't an extension of deity contradicts what we call new age thinking. Pantheism is infecting our culture in all sorts of ways. Remember the pop song that suggests looking for the hero inside yourself – the one that will lead to the key to your life? That is a clever way of saying the key to life is the hero within, the god inside us. It's not a transcendent God out there, distinct from his creation, but a god within. But this passage in Colossians subtly tells us that we are not part of God. It reminds us that God the Creator and his creation are distinct – though in Christ, as we shall see, marvellously joined and intertwined.

- *What damage would it do to our faith and theology if we believed that Christ was a created being? What other truths does this contradict?*

- *Looking for the hero within yourself, the god inside, is a popular message in today's culture. Share examples of the places and situations where this message is promoted.*

Christ and creation

In verse 16 Paul tells us that Jesus is the Creator. Through the Uncreated Son, the Father creates all there is. Note how comprehensive that creation is: 'For by him, all things were created: things in heaven and on earth, visible and invisible, whether thrones or powers or rulers or authorities; all things were created by him and for him.' Christ is at once the starting point and the goal of creation.

Why is the created universe here? Astonishingly, it is here for Christ! This was a sharp reminder for the church at Colosse. This ancient church was being threatened by principalities and powers, by superstition and occult practices, and it was riddled with fear. Paul says, look, when you belong to Christ, you are safe — this is your Father's world, your Saviour's creation. His point is that whatever powers there may be, visible or invisible — and some commentators think that these are not just spiritual powers, but in our day, for instance, are power structures of society, multi-national companies, global conglomerates, economic forces, international politics, the whole structure and fabric of the world — Christ is ultimately the Lord of them all. This passage is saying that wherever you look in space and time and things visible, or if you could see them, invisible, Jesus Christ has authority over them because he is the Lord. In this amazing universe of stars and planets, black holes, pulsars, quarks, deep space, parallel universes, whatever we could mention, imagine or discover — Jesus is before all of these, and in him and for him all these things were created. There is nothing outside of the majestic reign and sway of Christ.

What holds the whole universe together? What is the glue of creation? What is it that makes it all hang together, rather than hang loose? Verse 17 'and in him all things hold together.' Christ is the sustainer of the whole of the creation; he is what prevents the cosmos collapsing into a chaos! The Son of God, he is the glue of creation! How dare we think that Jesus is just for us Christians? No, he is the Lord, the magnificent ruler of all the whole universe, everything we can see, however far our telescopes can penetrate, and everything we cannot see, however profound and mysterious. Jesus Christ is Lord of all. The test of good theology is doxology, turning our thoughts into worship. Caroline Maria Noel's *At the Name of Jesus* captures this theology brilliantly:

> At his voice creation
> Sprang at once to sight,
> All the angel faces,
> All the hosts of light;
> Thrones and dominations,

Stars upon their way,
All the heavenly orders
In their great array.

- *What evidence do you see of powers opposed to Christ and his work in the world in:*

  - *Global companies?*
  - *International politics?*
  - *The structure of society?*

- *No matter what advances we make in medical science, nuclear physics, genetic testing etc, we will never surpass God's knowledge or his control. Should this spur us in to make more advances? Do we need to put any boundaries in place if God's control is limitless?*

- *Look back over the key verses and your answers to the questions. Summarise all the elements that make Christ king of creation. How does this assure us that we can depend on Christ as sufficient for our lives?*

Further study

- *We were described as being made in the image of God at creation (Gen. 1:26). What does that mean? How much of that image was lost in the fall? How is it being restored (see Col. 3:10)?*

Reflection and response

Christ's control of creation reminds us that he is in control of our lives – he has a plan for us even when we think things are going wrong! Give time for each person to find another verse in the Bible that reminds us that God is in control of our lives. Write it down and give it to someone else in your group. Meditate on the verse you've been given throughout the week.

Chapter 5 – Head of the church

Aim: To depend on Christ's sufficiency because he is head of the church

Focus on the theme

Share together your experiences of bosses – someone in charge of you at work, at university or even at home! What makes some experiences positive and others negative? How do you flourish when you have someone dependable in charge? Think about how Christ's headship makes us flourish as individuals and as a church.

Read: Colossians 1:15-29
Key verses: Colossians 1:18-20

Christ the head of the church

Colosse was a small town in the Lycus valley. Here Christians were under threat, under pressure, their backs to the wall. It is like many of us in our small fellowships, fearing the surrounding culture is going to overwhelm us and sink the church. But Paul reminds the Colossians that although they live in Colosse, they are also in Christ. Therefore, they are part of God's eternal purposes. God has written them into the great musical score of the ages that will ultimately bring his symphony of grace to the present cacophony of our world. Since they are part of God's church, they matter, they are vital. God's church is an outpost in time of God's everlasting kingdom. The church points to that glorious kingdom, when all shall be well. It is here in time as a foretaste and a pointer to Christ. The church is his body and he its head. Verse 18, 'And he is the head of the body, the church; he is the beginning and the firstborn from among the dead.'

Do you know about the 'Peter Principle'? Tom Peters is an American management guru who coined the phrase the 'Peter Principle'. In essence, the principle states that people keep getting promoted until they reach the level of their incompetence. How does it apply to Jesus Christ? Is he up to the job of running the church? Is he big enough? Or has he – I say it tremblingly – been promoted to the level of his incompetence as the head of the church?

Let me put it this way. The one who runs the church does that alongside running the whole universe! Millions of people in the church cannot be so arduous a challenge as sustaining billions of planets in who knows how many universes beyond our own. We forget too easily that Jesus runs the whole universe. He is the Lord God Almighty. He is the head of the church. That is a challenge for those of us who thought we were in charge of the churches we serve. God, of course, raises up leaders. But we are not indispensable. If you feel you are, your problem is theological. You don't believe in the Trinity, you believe in the 'quadrinity', to coin a phrase. You have joined the Godhead! But Paul tells us here that Christ is the cause and the source of the church's life. It is as the church stays connected to the head, as his body, that she draws from him all she needs to tough it out in difficult situations. The church has one foundation, Jesus Christ her Lord, and one head and supreme governor, the One who runs the universe. Is anyone else out there competent to be the church's head and sustainer? Only omnipotence need apply!

- *What can do we do, what safeguards can we put in place, to ensure that Jesus is, in practice, the head of our church?*

● *How does knowing that Jesus is head of our church help us deal with differences, splits and disagreements among the body of Christ?*

● *Christ is the head of the church but he has also given us earthly leaders. If we think our leaders are not keeping Christ as the head of the church, what constructive measures should we take? What should we not do?*

● *How would you deal with the following situations if they were happening in your own church?*

  ● *The church is looking for a Youth Pastor. The leaders have interviewed and are recommending a candidate to the church. You have not seen this young man with the young people but just don't feel he is right for the job.*
  ● *The church leaders have decided that all those involved in ministry should attend a training course. The course is run one night a week for six weeks. You feel that those involved in ministry are too busy already and that the leaders don't appreciate this.*
  ● *A new minister has decided to change the church constitution so that baptism by immersion is the norm. You have theological reasons for disagreeing with him and think he is unwise to make such a radical change so early in his tenure. What action should you take?*

We are also told that Christ is also the fullness of God, 'For God was pleased to have all his fullness dwell in him' (v19). This is the Christmas story. This is the scandal of particularity for Christianity. Christians insist that in this one solitary, unique life, we truly meet our Creator God, Jesus, Immanuel – God with us. We believe that the almighty, infinite, personal God stepped into this little tiny speck of inter-stellar dust, our Earth, in an obscure galaxy, to redeem us. The almighty Creator

God has come to us in Christ. The eighteenth century hymn-writer, Charles Wesley, captures the wonder splendidly:

> Let earth and heaven combine,
> Angels and men agree,
> To praise in songs divine
> The incarnate Deity;
> Our God contracted to a span,
> Incomprehensibly made man.

Christ and the cross

Christ is also the firstborn from the dead. If verse 19 reminds us of the Christmas story, then verses 18, 20, 22, tell us the Easter one. 'Through him to reconcile all things to himself, making peace through his blood, shed on the cross' (v20). What is 'blood' in Scripture? Here it speaks of a life given in death, a violent, sacrificial death. Elsewhere, we are reminded that 'without the shedding of blood, there is no forgiveness' (Heb. 9:22). Here is the cross. For the first three or four centuries, Christians dared not use the symbol of the cross. They knew what it meant: it was a horror, it was a place of immense torture and pain. They could not use that symbol of the cross, as we use it today, until the memory of the awfulness of crucifixion had died out in the Roman Empire. But the purpose of the cross was understood:

> He died that we might be forgiven,
> He died to make us good,
> That we might go at last to heaven,
> Saved by His precious blood.

> There was no other good enough
> To pay the price of sin;

He only could unlock the gate
Of heaven, and let us in.
      Cecil Frances Alexander

How desperate our sin must be if there was no other solution than the eternal Son of God coming from the throne of the universe to redeem us. And how do we know it is true? Because 'he is the first-born from among the dead'; literally, 'out of the dead' (v18). Here is the resurrection. Christians don't believe that Jesus just came back as a ghost, or reappeared for a while, resuscitated like Lazarus in John 11. True enough, Lazarus died and was raised again. However, the problem with poor old Lazarus was this: like the widow of Nain's son, or Jairus' daughter, he had to go and do his dying all over again! You and I live and die. The difference with Christ is that he died and now lives forever in the power of an endless life: 'Since Christ was raised from the dead, he cannot die again' (Rom. 6:9).

Do you know anybody else in that category? Do you know any other great philosopher, politician, economist, educator or religious leader, who has died and is now alive in the power of an endless life? Jesus alone is the firstborn from the dead. But here is the great news: because he is 'the firstborn from the dead', the first to rise from the dead in an endless life, thank God he isn't the last. He is the forerunner of many others. We are going to be raised in power also! He, the living Christ, will raise us too: 'Because I live, you also will live' is his promise (Jn. 14:19).

● *How would you explain to a non-Christian why no one else but Jesus could die for our sins? Why did blood have to be shed to cleanse sins?*

All things

Christ is also the Reconciler: 'And through him to reconcile to himself all things' (v20). Note, it isn't all 'men', or 'people' here.

The Greek is neuter. It is 'all things.' 'To reconcile to himself all things whether things on earth or things in heaven, by making peace through his blood, shed on the cross.' One of the early church Fathers, Origen, believed in what is called universalism – that there would come a time when Christ would literally turn back the clock on sin in such a way that not only would everybody be saved, but even the devil himself would be redeemed. This brand of universalism has only ever been a minority belief in the Christian church. That is significant. For the Bible does not teach, though some wish it did, that regardless of repentance and faith in Christ, at the end of time everybody from St Francis of Assisi through to Adolf Hitler, everybody, whether they want to be or not, will be saved.

What does it mean for Christ to reconcile all things to himself? I believe it teaches that the death of Christ atones for the sins of people, and puts us right with God. In addition, in the death and resurrection of Christ, God is reversing the curse that is on the world, and through Christ he is going to bring in a whole new cosmos, 'a new heaven and a new earth, the home of righteousness' (2 Pet. 3:13). This is the thrust of Romans 8:19-21. Phillips puts it so well in his translation, 'the whole creation is on tiptoe to see the wonderful sight of the sons of God, coming into their own.' There is going to be a whole new created sphere where 'the wolf will live with the lamb … and the young child put his hand into the viper's nest', in a world full of the knowledge of the Lord (Is. 11:6-9).

Does that mean that ultimately everybody and everything, every demon, the devil himself, will ultimately be brought back to how things were before sin entered the world? Well, this isn't peace amongst equals. Philippians 2:10-11 tells us that, 'At the name of Jesus every knee should bow, in heaven and on earth, and under the earth, and every tongue confess that Jesus Christ is Lord.' So, does that mean everybody becomes a Christian? No. But everybody now realises the *status quo* in the universe. That is, in this universe and whatever is beyond it, everywhere in the whole cosmos, Jesus Christ is Lord. A Christian is someone who believes and acts on that truth now. At the end of time, everybody will believe and confess it. When the Second World War came to a conclusion and peace was declared, those who had been the perpetrators of vast crimes against humanity were brought to war tribunals to answer for what they had done. They may have continued to detest and be absolutely defiant towards the Allies before whom they had stood. But their power had been fully negated, and they were now reconciled to the status quo: they had lost. This is what I believe Paul is talking about here. Willingly or unwillingly, every knee will bow to Jesus as Saviour or Judge.

- *How should knowing that everyone will not become a Christian in the end affect your personal evangelism?*

Jesus the centre

Finally, in this section we are reminded that Jesus is the Pre-eminent One: 'he is the head of the body, the church; he is the beginning, the firstborn from the dead, so that in everything he may have the supremacy' (v18). He is pre-eminent and peerless in every realm. What Jesus Christ, as the Son of God, is eternally in the heart of God, he becomes in actuality in space and time because he becomes one of us. Similarly, Philippians 2:5-11 reminds us that the One who from all eternity was God and Lord, through his death and rising again, is proclaimed Lord before all the universe. He, who was before all things, has the pre-eminence in all things. A recent song expresses it well when it encourages us to make Jesus the centre, the source, the light of our lives since he already is the centre of the universe. We need to live our lives with that reality – and seek to approximate our homes, churches, communities and world to that truth. Jesus, be the centre. Is he pre-eminent? This is the

unsurpassed Jesus, to whom we are to yield the pre-eminent
place in and over all of our lives.

- *What practical steps, as individuals and as a group, could we take
  to ensure Christ remains the centre of our lives?*

Further study

*The false teachers told the Colossians that they had not yet enjoyed the
fullness of spiritual experience. So Paul deliberately sets out to show
that Christ was full of God, and now the Colossians are full of Christ.
He did not want them to search for new experiences outside Christ
because everything they needed was to be found in their relationship
with him. Trace Paul's use of the words fullness, full, and fill throughout Colossians to see his line of argument.*

Reflection and response

*Share communion together. As you do so, remember what it cost for us
to be reconciled to God. Reflect that through Christ's death we became
part of the body of Christ of which he is the head. Take time quietly to
confess any area in your lives where you have not given him the pre-
eminence.*

Chapter 6 – Lord of my life

Aim: To depend on Christ's power because he wants to be Lord of my life

Focus on the theme

Draw a picture of a house and label all the different rooms. Use each room to describe a different aspect of your Christian life. For example, the utility room could be the service you do, the bedroom could be your devotional times with the Lord. In which area is it hardest to invite Christ to be Lord? Are there any rooms where you have barred him from entry?

Read: Colossians 1:15-29
Key verses: Colossians 1:21-29

Free from accusation

In the nineteenth century, Karl Marx used a word that, in the twentieth century, became the basis for communism which cost millions their lives. That word was alienation. He believed workers had been alienated from the fruit of their labours by the exploitation of their capitalist bosses. So far as the Bible is concerned, there is a far deeper alienation – an exploitation by sin that alienates us from God and each other. These verses remind us what God has done about it. Though 'alienated from God' (v21), now in Christ we have been 'reconciled' (v22). Jesus has died so that 'he might present you holy in his

presence without blemish and free from accusation' (v22). Isn't
that fantastic? Christ has died so you can be free from that
gnawing accusation, that conscience that is always twisting
you this way and that. In addition, there is the 'accuser of the
brothers' as Revelation 12 describes the devil. But Christ has
died for us and as we surrender to him, we are presented free
from accusation. As the final verse of Wesley's hymn *And can it
be?* puts it, 'No condemnation now I dread.' No longer alienated, reconciled; no longer guilty, free from accusation.
Fantastic!

● *We know that Christ died to free us from condemnation but at
times we can still feel the accuser on our backs. How can we make
freedom in Christ more of a reality in our daily lives?*

● *Being presented 'holy in his sight, without blemish and free from
accusation' is dependent on 'if you continue in your faith' (v23).
A young Christian in your church has just read these verses and
is worried because they have had a relapse into some particular
area of sin. How would you explain the meaning of these verses
to them?*

Suffering for the gospel

Verse 24 calls us to suffer for him. 'I rejoice in what was suffered
for you, and I fill up in my flesh what is still lacking in regard to
Christ's afflictions, for the sake of his body, which is the church.'
At first reading, it sounds as if Paul is a co-redeemer here. But
no, it means this: Paul is prepared to suffer for the gospel he
believes in so that others may come to know Christ. God only
ever had one Son without sin, but he actually has no sons or
daughters without suffering. For others to hear the gospel, some
will suffer a great deal. Some pay the ultimate price.

There was a little Welsh girl, Mary Fisher, who had the face and voice of an angel. She was one of my co-students at London Bible College in the early 1970s. One evening, she came with Alistair Begg, now a renowned Keswick speaker, and me to take a service at a Rescue Mission in London's Webber Street. The lads, the tramps and down-and-outs, gave Alistair and me a rough ride! But she had these guys eating out of her hand – just by singing the songs of Christ to them. She went off to be a missionary with the Elim Church to what was then Rhodesia, now Zimbabwe.

In June 1978, she and another dozen missionaries and their children were brutally butchered to death by the Freedom Fighters. A friend of mine, Stan Hannan, a chaplain with the Rhodesian Army, was one of the first on the scene of that dreadful and literal carnage. In fact, all the birds and animals had fled from the area, as if nature itself was revolted by this wickedness. Stan told me, 'You could feel the air heavy with evil.' Mary had actually survived for a couple of days. 'Thank God', said Stan, 'that the Lord took her home', such were the appalling injuries inflicted on that girl with the face of an angel. Subsequently, the troops found her cassette player. On it was a song she had been teaching the children of the mission school to sing: 'For me to live is Christ, to die is gain.' Some time later, when the guerrilla war was over, some of those terrorists had come to Christ. 'The blood of the martyrs is the seed of the Church,' said the Early Church Father, Tertullian. See what Jesus says in John 12:24.

'When Jesus calls us to follow him', says Dietrich Bonhoeffer, 'it is a call to come and die.' Some Christians pay the ultimate price for following Jesus. All Christians are called to pay something to follow the crucified, so that others may hear the gospel. Some words from Amy Carmichael challenge me deeply. The piece is entitled, *No Scar?*

Hast thou no scar?
No hidden scar on foot, or side, or hand?

I hear thee sung as mighty in the land,
I hear them hail thy bright ascendant star,
Hast thou no scar?

Hast thou no wound?
Yet I was wounded by the archers, spent,
Leaned Me against a tree to die; and rent
By ravening beasts that compassed Me, I swooned:
Hast thou no wound?

No wound? no scar?
Yet, as the Master shall the servant be,
And piercèd are the feet that follow Me;
But thine are whole: can he have followed far
Who has nor wound nor scar?

Amy Carmichael, Towards Jerusalem, *(CLC)*

● *What suffering for the gospel do we experience in the UK?
Besides death, what other costs do Christians face in following
Jesus? Be specific!*

A servant of the gospel

To paraphrase a line of a hymn, 'If we suffer with our Lord
below, we will reign with him above'! In the meantime, we are
called to serve him (v25-27). Paul says he has found his niche,
he knows what he is built for and called to: 'I have become a
servant of the gospel.' That is a call to each one of us, to be
a servant of the gospel wherever God has placed us, in that old
folks' home or hi-tech company. For some of us this call
becomes so persistent that it becomes a calling to full-time
service at home or overseas. You perhaps? Whatever and wherever, we are called to share the gospel, as verses 28-29 say: 'We
proclaim him, admonishing and teaching everyone in all

wisdom, so we may present everyone, perfect (mature), in Christ. To this end I labour, struggling with all his energy, which so powerfully works in me.'

- *Being a servant of the gospel isn't only about being able to explain the way of salvation to people. In addition, can we be servants of the gospel in our:*

  - *Work places?*
  - *Homes?*
  - *Churches?*

- *What difference does/should it make that we are servants of the gospel in a missionary situation today in Britain? Should we present the gospel any differently from the past, use any different resources?*

- *Explain what Paul's aim is when he says he wants to 'present everyone perfect in Christ' (v28).*

His sovereignty: my sufficiency

Paul, how do you do it? How do you keep on suffering, how do you keep on serving? How do you keep on investing in kingdom work without quitting? We need to go back to (v27) – 'To them God has chosen to make known among the Gentiles the glorious riches of this mystery, *which is Christ in you.*'

One of the benefits of having had a little boy at home, my grandson, is that you get to watch children's films with a good conscience! One of my old heroes, *Spiderman*, has recently had a new lease of life in a Hollywood film of that name. Do you know how he became Spiderman? He got bitten by a radioactive spider and since then he has been hanging around everywhere! In other words, the effect of that bite – sure, I know it is fiction! – is that he has powers, abilities and capacities that he never had before! If I can put it reverently, when I am bitten by this Lord of glory, the Supreme Governor of his church, and the Lord of the universe, when I am in touch with him, when Christ is in me, then I have abilities and resources I did not have before. Jesus is *for* me, *with* me and *in* me. His sovereignty is my sufficiency. Christ the Lord of glory, by his Spirit, in you! We need to speak less about our problems and inadequacies, and so much more of the sufficiency of the One who has all the power in the universe to present us and all his church, holy and without blemish before him, free from accusation.

- *Christ's lordship in our lives means freedom from condemnation and the prospect of glory, but it also means suffering and servant-hood. Where else in the Bible do we learn that suffering and servanthood are part of our calling?*

- *Paul presents his suffering and servanthood as normal in the Christian life. Is this an encouragement or discouragement to you?*

- *We don't always feel like we have the living Christ empowering us. What practical steps can we take to be more aware of his presence and to rely on his power?*

Reflection and response

Meditate on the truth, 'his sovereignty is my sufficiency.' Write down on a piece of paper the areas of your life, the problems and needs you have, where you want to invite Christ to be Lord. Draw a throne on top of what you have written signalling your willingness to let Christ reign. Perhaps you could throw your sheets of paper into a wastepaper basket or burn them on an open fire, to symbolise your break with the past and Christ's new lordship of the situation.

Review Colossians 1:15-29

Read over Colossians 1:15-29 again. Paul is expounding the theme that Jesus is sufficient for us because of his supremacy over creation and the church. He is also sufficient for us because of the salvation he offers through his work on the cross and the purpose he brings to our lives when we follow him. He truly is Lord of all!

As a group, think of as many phrases as you can to describe Christ – they can be phrases from the Bible or truths you have learnt from your own experience. Make a big list – this can be your own hymn that you can say or sing out to God as a group. Spend an extended time in worship, thanking God for who Jesus is and all that he has done for us.

Points to Ponder

- *What have you learnt about God?*
- *What have you learnt about yourself?*
- *What actions or attitudes do you need to change as a result?*

Chapter 7 – A deeper knowledge

Aim: To press on towards a deeper knowledge of Christ that we can live out in daily life

Focus on the theme

There are many things that compete with our desire to know Christ better. There are many subtle temptations. Look through a range of magazines and newspapers and come up with evidence of the alternative spiritualities that vie for our attention.

Read: Colossians 2:1-23
Key verses: Colossians 2:1-7

Principalities and powers

In the western world, many believe, if there is a God, he is 'up there' in some kind of supra-mundane, supernatural realm. He is beyond us, a far away God. And here in *our* world, the *real* world, we get on with life on the natural level. We hardly expect, even as Christians, for God miraculously to intervene in the real world of sense perception.

The situation is very different when you go to other parts of the world. In other cultures, many believe that there isn't only a supreme God up there and a natural world down here. In between, there are whole hierarchies and tiers of authorities, principalities, powers and various kinds of spirits who dominate people's lives. Until recently, we in the western world tended to exclude this middle tier. But in the last two or three decades, there has been a massive change in the way many western people view the world. Indeed, we are in a time when people, some of them very sophisticated, often opt for one or more of the alternative spiritualities on offer and which are believed to occupy this middle ground, this middle tier, between a supreme God and the world in which we live. So reading of tarot cards, having one's aura purified or visiting sites of harmonic convergence to get in sync with powerful earth forces have become respectable. Mother gods and earth goddesses are in vogue.

Here in Colossians 2, Paul confronted a world full of elemental spirits, spirits that many believed controlled their lives and needed to be respected and placated. But he offers hope by explaining why Christians don't need to be controlled by these powers. In Christ there is freedom from such bondage and fullness of life. A deepening knowledge of Christ is what these Colossians needed. Paul reminds them that he has been labouring on their behalf, struggling for them (v1). He struggles in his prayers for them; he struggles in his writing for them; he is concerned that they grow and mature and are not put off course by the false teaching that is threatening their church and the one at Laodicea (v1).

How do we reach that point of freedom and sufficiency in Christ? First of all, we are to be encouraged in heart (v2). Do you know anybody who has died from too much encouragement? No? Neither do I! We don't actually need friendly churches. We need churches where people discover friends. There is a difference. In friendly churches you get a nice warm welcome and that is it. Bye! Nobody ever invites you home, nobody takes you out for a coffee, nobody offers to baby-sit or help with the ironing. All we can say is, 'what a nice, friendly, warm church welcome!' But we need more than friendly churches. We need encouraging communities of people being transformed to be like Jesus. Paul adds, 'united in love' (v2). Churches that view love as an optional extra have forgotten their identity. Does not the Bible teach 'the greatest of these is – love' (1 Cor. 13:13)?

● *What do you think an encouraging church looks like? Describe the formal events and informal relationships that must take place.*

● *Which of these measures do you think your church most needs to become more encouraging rather than just friendly?*

Love and understanding

Notice that there is a purpose for this love – it is so that they may have the 'full riches of complete understanding' (v2). He wants them to be Christians who are full of love, but also Christians who grow in their faith intellectually so they appreciate all they have in Jesus. If only we could put these two things together! In my experience, you sometimes meet groups of Christians who are very loving but they seem unable to think coherently and biblically about their faith in the world. At the other extreme, I recently heard of a church where somebody asked whether the banquet in Luke 14 was going to be held on the earth or in the air. Interesting? Perhaps. Who cares? This church cared so much that it had a six way split over it! Beggars belief, doesn't it? Some Christians have been deeply traumatised by splits in their church over trivial issues. Folk took a hard line on something that was much ado about nothing. Pharisees always major on minors. We need Christians who love God with all their minds and hearts – and their neighbours, too!

● *How do we balance love and complete understanding? In other words, how do we promote growth in our hearts as well as our heads?*

Paul continues, 'I want you to have complete understanding.' Why? So you may become a wise guy and a smart Alec? No – in order that you may know the 'mystery of God' (v2) Now that is a tricky word for us. We think of a mystery as a puzzle. But mystery in the New Testament means something rather different. A mystery is something God had hinted at in one way and another, but now has clearly revealed. And no one could have guessed what God was about; it is as if he kept his cards close to his chest all through the Old Testament, yet kept dropping hints. The mystery was that, right from the very beginning, God did not simply intend to make only the Jewish race his chosen people. Rather his Plan A was to bring salvation to the whole world. To everybody. The Jews' election and special status was for a purpose. Through them salvation would come through Christ to bless the world.

Why is it important to know about the mystery? Because that mystery is Christ. The whole Old Testament was and still is pointing forwards to him. He is the key to unlocking its treasures and to understanding what its big picture is all about. Indeed, he is the key to life itself, the one in whom are 'hidden all the treasures of wisdom and knowledge' (v3). When we get Christ, we have hit the jackpot. He is what everything is ultimately about – life, the universe and everything else! Just think of that. Christ is what the very structure of reality is all about.

- *Look at Galatians 3:8, 1 Peter 1:1-12. These verses show us the glimpses of the mystery throughout the Old Testament.*

- *Paul's aim is that the Colossians 'know the mystery of God, namely, Christ.' What does it mean to know Christ? What kind of knowledge is it? Are there any other helpful Bible references to explain this word 'know'?*

- *Verse 3 says in Christ 'are hidden all the treasures of wisdom and knowledge.' Does this mean we should not look for or accept truth we find in:*

  - *Self-help books – on parenting for example?*
  - *Other religions?*

Jesus: all we ever need

Paul is saying that all that could be anticipated elsewhere, all that could be longed for by the human heart, can be found in Jesus, it is all in him. He continues, 'I tell you this so that no-one may deceive you by fine sounding arguments. For though I am absent from you in body, I am present with you in spirit and delight to see how orderly you are and how firm your faith in Christ is' (v4, 5). Here is strong, robust faith, assured of its resources in Christ, the Christ who is sufficient for every situation. If that is so, then there is no need to turn to other spirits to help you. That is the great curse of syncretism – you take a little of this faith, that religion and the other spirituality. It was afflicting the Colossian church. Yes by all means, ran the argument, have Jesus – but you also need help from this spirit, that demi-god and the other idol. But if you are bound up with Jesus; in him, as Lord, you will discover all you will ever need.

In a syncretistic, pluralistic world, not unlike the Colossians' world, we are called to grow and develop in Christ. Verse 6 'So then, just as you received Christ Jesus as Lord, continue to live in him.' The word 'live' is literally 'walk' – 'I want you to walk in Christ.' Walk in his footsteps. Then Paul mixes his metaphors a little. He says 'I want you to be like a tree, well-rooted, or like a house, built up.' In other words, these are pictures of stability, growth and development.

I remember the date precisely – 24th December, 1978. A visitor to East London Tabernacle Baptist Church, of which I was Pastor, came out of the service. She had noted the birth three days before of our first child, Paul Stephen, weighing in at a mere 5lbs 7oz, less that two and a half kilos. The visitor looked at me and remarked, 'He isn't very big, is he?' How dare she! That's my boy! I am over six feet tall, and was towering over her when I replied, 'I was only 6lbs 8oz (less than three kilos), and look what happened to me!' If you could see my son now, he's got muscles where I haven't got places! Why? Because he's grown. He's developed! Paul says to these Christians, 'It is great to be in Christ, but don't have an arrested development. Now you have got to grow in him. Grow up in your faith. Grow up in your salvation!'

● *What other pictures could we use to describe Christian growth?*

An attitude of gratitude

It is tragic when you see folk whose physical growth has been hindered for whatever reason. But it is more tragic when we have been Christians for a while and yet have remained spiritual babes. There are Christians who are still in spiritual kindergarten, a spiritual Peter Pan in a Never-Never land of spiritual adolescence. Paul says: 'I don't want you to be like that, I want you to grow up.'

Do you notice, 'rooted ... in the faith as you were taught', and 'overflowing with thankfulness'? Thankfulness – an attitude of gratitude. A lot of Christians I know live, at least metaphorically, up in Cumbria. They live just north of Keswick. It is only a little village but there are many Christians I know who live there. Do you know what the name of the village is? You may have passed through it. It is called 'Unthank.' I came through it the other day. Are you living in Unthank, with no gratitude, with no thankfulness? Are you cynical? There are some people who approach me, and I am thinking, 'For what I am about to receive, may the Lord make me truly thankful.' They are negative, they are carping, they are bitter. The first words out of their mouths are always criticism.

When we are like that, we are grieving the Spirit of God. We must be great fun to live with! Unthankfulness is a great sin. It will bring misery to your own life, misery to your home, to your church, to the place where you work and where you chill out. Be overflowing with thanksgiving. Don't live in Unthank – the world has enough problems already!

- *Why are we so often lacking in thanksgiving?*

- *In twos, reread Colossians 2:1-7. Note down on an A4 sheet all the markers that show someone is pressing on towards a deeper knowledge of Christ.*

Reflection and response

Cut up everyone's sheets so that there is one statement per piece of paper. Scatter all the papers in the middle of the room and have each member of the group come and take a piece of paper that has on it the area in which they most need to grow. Take some time for personal reflection. Then pray for your church and the areas it most needs to grow.

Chapter 8 – Remember your freedom

Aim: Beware of deceptive philosophies by remembering the freedom won for you on the Cross

Focus on the theme

Take the Pepsi Challenge! Blindfold someone in your group and get them to decide which drink is Pepsi and which is Coca-Cola. Start thinking in terms of the spiritual realm. What is the real thing and how do we discern it?

Read: Colossians 2:1-23
Key verses: Colossians 2:8-15

Beware of imitations

Paul warns us: 'See to it that no-one takes you captive through hollow and deceptive philosophy' (v6-8). Firstly, please note that there is nothing wrong with philosophy, with understanding how people think. Paul isn't dismissing philosophy *per se*, a genuine love of wisdom, which is what the word literally means. But he is talking about sham philosophy which depends, he says, 'on human tradition and the basic principles of this world rather than on Christ' (v8). He is telling us to beware of being deceived by imitations.

My son and I were in Hong Kong recently. He wanted to go to the street market because he was looking for a watch. On

one of the stalls, the vendor shiftily looked around and produced something from under the counter – a Rolex watch.
Twenty pounds! Was it the real thing? Well, it didn't last too long
when we got it home! It was a genuine imitation. It looked like
the real thing, but it was a cheap fake.

Now, says Scripture, don't let anyone do that to you with
your faith. Do not let anyone deceive you with hollow and
deceptive philosophy. It is like the MGM studios where you
can visit a film set and see these fine fronted mansions. Then
you go and look behind them and they are just frontage.
There is no substance. There are deceptive philosophies that
capture people's minds and the way they think; they are hollow and deceptive because they are based either on human
tradition – ancient wisdom passed down from who knows
where – or on the basic principles of this world. The basic
principles might refer to wind, earth, fire, and water – the
four basic elements the ancients believed in. But I think, in
this context, Paul is particularly talking about the magical
powers that were prevalent everywhere in the ancient world.
The problem with these spiritual realities in the middle tier,
of which we spoke earlier, is that they are not based 'on
Christ.' Literally, they are not 'according to Christ.' What is
wrong with these alternative spiritualities, these new age
philosophies in which there is actually nothing particularly
new? Paul says their fatal flaw is this – they do not depend on
Christ. They exclude him, ignore him, or domesticate him by
adding him to their pantheon. Him! The Lord of the
Universe! How dare they!

● *How do we look out for imitations? Brainstorm what criteria you
would give a new Christian or young person going off to college
for the first time, to help them decide whether a church, philosophy, or individuals were 'based on Christ'?*

The Word became flesh

In contrast to all these shams, 'in Christ all the fullness of the Deity lives in bodily form' (v9). Notice the phrase, 'all the Deity.' Note that it isn't just a quality of 'divineness', as you and I can be godlike, or angels can be godlike. In Jesus, I do not find a sham deity or an approximation to deity but actually I meet God himself. Paul goes on to say this Deity 'lives in bodily form.' Here again is the astonishing story of Christmas and the astonishing story of the gospel. The eternal God has joined the human race, he has become one of us, to seek and to save us. And he did it by coming into a virgin's womb.

Some Christians profess problems with belief in the virgin birth, or more precisely, the virgin conception. Have you ever wondered why God chose to enter the human race that way? Here is at least one angle on it. Christians believe that when a child is conceived in the womb, at that point in time, a new person who did not exist before comes into existence. But Christians believe that when Jesus was conceived in the womb, it was not a new person coming into existence at all. It was entirely appropriate, therefore, that his conception was unique and miraculous because the one who came to Mary's womb existed from all eternity, as God the Son. That is an astonishing claim. Into this tiny grain of sand that we call our Earth, on this vast seashore of the universe, God has personally come. 'The Word became flesh and dwelt amongst us' (Jn. 1:14).

What's more, Paul says, all the fulness *'lives* in bodily form', not *'lived.'* Christians believe that the Jesus who became one of us is still one of us. He has joined a human nature to his divine nature and he is one person, God and man, still, forever. So, 'there is one God and one mediator between God and men, the man Christ Jesus' (1 Tim. 2:5). There is a man at God's right hand today; there is someone who has taken our human nature to the very throne of God. Some people think about the size of the universe and ask, 'Do we matter?' The gospel says, 'Oh, we matter infinitely, because God in Christ has personally come to seek and to save people like us.' And he became one of us to do so!

- *Is it vital to believe in the virgin birth in order to be a Christian?*

- *Why is it important that Jesus is still a man in heaven today? Why did he not shed his humanity when he left earth?*

Dead, buried and raised

Why did he do it? Why did Jesus come to earth? Because 'you were dead in your sins' (v13). People were made in the image of God, made for a love relationship with him. But because of our sinfulness, through our moral failure, we are now alienated from God, so much so that we are, in God's sight, spiritually dead. We are out of relationship with him. We were dead but now we have been 'buried with Christ in baptism' (v12). What the apostle is speaking about here is not so much the methods or moments of baptism, though they are not excluded. Rather, it is the spiritual transformation whereby, through the death of Christ, his death counts for me and my sins are dealt with and buried with him. Then notice, 'you have been raised to life in him' (v12), or similarly, 'God made you alive with Christ' (v13). What does Christ bring us? He brings us spiritual new life. He brings the life of God into the soul of a man or a woman. Through faith in Christ I live again, I am born again, I am changed, I am transformed, eternal life becomes mine, because of the saving grace of Christ.

Whenever I sit on a plane before take off, I look at the tons of metal and people, and everything in me tells me that this thing cannot fly. After all, there is a thing called the law of gravity. But, at a certain point, as that plane zips along the runway and the aerofoils are tilted, suddenly it leaves the ground and we begin to fly. What has happened to the law of gravity? If it has been suspended, we are hanging from the ceiling. No, it is still in operation. It has not been suspended so much as superseded as we take to the skies. I have at that point come under another law, a higher law, the law of aerodynamics – I am flying! What does Christ do for me that no one else can do? He comes and he takes me beyond my law of gravity, the law of sin and death, and by his grace he makes me fly by the 'law of aerodynamics' – the Spirit of God.

- *How do these word-pictures help us grasp the enormity of what Christ did for us on the cross:*

    - *Death to life?*
    - *Baptism?*
    - *Circumcision?*

IOU

In Christ, all our sins have been dealt with, in Christ they have all been paid on the nail, literally. Verse 14 tells us that Christ 'cancelled the written code, with its regulations that were against us and stood opposed to us.' The written code here is like an IOU. I owe you so much money; I cannot pay it, so you have my IOU. In this case, it isn't money but a death warrant. My name is on it, I am condemned because of my sins, whose 'wages are death' (Rom. 6:23). And then, wonder of wonders, somebody comes and takes that death warrant with my name on it and nails it to a cross. Someone else underwrites my debt by paying my bill.

Right at the heart of the Christian faith is this concept of forgiveness. If I owe you a hundred pounds, I am in your debt. If you forgive me, then who has stood the bill? You have! The person who forgives pays the bill. People think forgiveness is easy until they have to forgive. They think it is easy for God. But it isn't. If God is to forgive he must personally underwrite the bill. That is why Christians believe God was in Christ reconciling the world to himself. The picture isn't that here, on one side, is an angry God, and on the other are poor sinners, and along comes this nice Jesus who says 'I will sort it for them.' No, it was 'God who so loved the world that he gave his one and only Son for us' (Jn. 3:16). The gospel does not tell me that the cross of Christ is something extrinsic to God, something that happened out there. Rather, it is something that has happened in the very heart of God, out of love, to forgive us sinners all our sins – 'God was in Christ, reconciling the world to himself' (2 Cor. 5:19).

Because Christ took our death warrant, we are set free. 'And having disarmed the powers and authorities, he made a public spectacle of them, triumphing over them by the cross' (v15). The powers and authorities did not know that in crucifying the Lord of glory they were not only fulfilling the plan, purpose and mystery of God. They were also overstretching themselves so that in the very death that Jesus died, he defeated them and robbed death of its power. Colosse was part of an ancient world riddled with superstition and magic, where threatening and terrifying evil spirits were believed to hold sway over people's lives. It was a world dominated by all sorts of magic potions and rituals. The apostle says, 'Look, in Christ, all that stuff has been met on the nail, for on the cross Jesus defeated the principalities and powers.' Rather than always looking to these principalities and powers for help, look to the cross where God in Christ meets us in grace and mercy.

● *Paul writes that evil has already been decisively defeated through the cross. This does not seem to be the case in our world and even in our own lives, so what is the status of evil today?*

- *What philosophies, past sins or difficulties are we as individuals prone to focus on rather than on the cross of Christ?*
- *What things are we asking people to think about or focus on when we say look to the cross of Christ'?*
- *In what practical ways can we remember the cross of Christ throughout the day? Share tips and ideas together.*

A friend of mine used to be a postman. I don't know how this happens, but dogs seem to have a canine committee resolution entitled, 'Let's get the postman', don't they? This friend used to deliver mail to a big house where they had a huge dog. Every time he opened the gate and walked onto the path, this dog used to romp towards him, growling, barking, snarling, going wild. Initially, he did not know what to do, until he noticed that the dog was on a big chain. But that was only half the story. The chain still allowed the dog a certain amount of freedom. However, it was limited. The dog on the chain could not reach the path. My friend discovered that, as long as he kept to the path, he was safe. But there is more to this story. You see, the chain did not actually keep the dog from the postman. It was what held the chain – a huge concrete stake in the ground. So, each morning when the postman entered the garden, he did not look at the dog, nor even its chain. He used to check just one thing. Was that chain still properly staked into the ground? Was the stake holding? Even when the dog was going wild with fury, my friend would check that the stake was holding. If it was, he was safe.

Every morning, as I go out into this dangerous world, I have to ask myself, is the stake of the cross holding in the ground? It is? Of course! If I therefore keep to the path of Christ, looking to his cross, I can walk in liberty, free from bondage, however ugly or terrifying the evil one seems to be. In Christ I am delivered, free.

Reflection and response

Watch the crucifixion scene from the Jesus film together. Reflect on what the cross meant for God the Father and God the Son. Picture yourself there in the crowd. Remember – because Jesus had a list of charges nailed to his cross, the charges against us have been cancelled!

Chapter 9 – Breaking with the past

Aim: To break with our past way of life, its values and practices

Focus on the theme

Share snapshots and videos of special family times. Videos give a much fuller picture of what actually happened, don't they? In our spiritual life, we are often concerned about the snapshots – looking right at a particular moment. But God is more interested in the video of our life – he is interested in long-term change, in our acting differently because our hearts and values have changed. Through his enabling we will be spiritually transformed.

Read: Colossians 2:1–23
Key verses: Colossians 2:16–23

Christ the only mediator

The rest of this chapter is all about superstition – charms, astrology, potions and spells. In the ancient world, whether you were a Gentile or in many cases even a Jew, when you had a problem – illness, disappointment in love, lack of money – you pieced together a list of the names of various angels and powers. You could pick and mix the names of Jewish angels with the names of God, and even with a whole pile of Gentile deities. This is syncretism. Then you called on all these power-ful beings to help you — that is what verse 18 is referring to. When Paul talks about the worship of angels, it isn't that they were necessarily worshipping angels, or mystically joining in the worship of the angels. Rather, it seems, people were calling on angels to come and assist them. And what the apostle is saying is, you do not have to call on other mediators, the only media-tor you need is Christ! No matter what you face, since all the treasures of wisdom and knowledge are in Jesus (see v3), you do not need to go anywhere else. Therefore you should not spend your time worrying whether you have doffed your cap to this particular power, paid your penance to that particular princi-pality or strayed into some evil spirit's territory. Paul says, we are in Christ, the great victor! You are set free from all such bondages.

Before I was a Christian, I was incredibly superstitious. I could see the sense of not walking under ladders, but there were all sorts of other things over which I was superstitious, especially as a football fan. You will find loads of sports fans are incredibly superstitious. They have to wear a special sort of tie or a pair of socks or a little amulet or something. But Paul says all that is totally inappropriate now you are a Christian. Christ washes all that away. And no matter how much people go on about their spiritual experiences (v18), such experience isn't self-authenti-cating. You have had a big spiritual experience? At one level, the Bible asks, so what? Are you pressing on with Christ? It isn't just spending time on the floor, or with your hands in the air, or whatever spiritually turns you on. Rather, it is spending time on your knees so you can walk with Christ day by day, that is what is important. Paul adds a warning — look out because otherwise people will load you down: 'You have got to do this, and you need to do that, and you have to have the other', and then it becomes a form of legalism and bondage. They tell you if you want to be really spiritual, then 'Do not handle! Do not touch! Do not taste!' this, that or the other (v21). All these little petty rules merely have an appearance of wisdom, but they cannot make us genuinely good or Christ-like (v23).

- *How do we as individuals hedge our bets? In what ways can we be superstitious rather than putting our full trust in Christ for this life and the next?*

- *What secular philosophies subtly find their way into church life?*

- *Verse 16 says 'Do not let anyone judge you...' We often judge each other on the snapshots that we see rather than the bigger video picture. Share some valid responses to the following scenarios:*

  - *A member of your home group says they don't have time to come to the group this week but you see them the following evening going into the pub with some non-Christian friends*
  - *You see the minister's wife going into Tesco on Sunday*
  - *One of the young professionals gives up a church ministry position because their work is too demanding. A few weeks later you learn that they have just accepted a significant salary rise and promotion.*

- *Paul says we should avoid superstition and legalism because 'the reality is found in Christ' (v17). What are the non-negotiables of a relationship with Christ? What activities and principles cannot be discarded?*

- *Verse 18 talks about the prize. What is the prize and how can others disqualify us from it?*

Do not get into bondage, Paul warns, rather stay connected (v19): 'He has lost connection with the Head, from whom the whole body, supported and held together by its ligaments and sinews, grows as God causes it to grow.' What is my biggest challenge every day? To stay in living, vital connection to Christ. How? One way is to notice the context here of the body, the church. It is with other Christians I grow and need to stay connected. There are some silly Christians who actually think they are going to make it to heaven with all guns blazing without the help of any other Christian.

I must have been about eight or nine years of age before I realised that my Dad had not single-handedly won the Second World War! The reason? He was captured at Dunkirk and he spent five years in a 'holiday camp' called Stalag 8b, as a prisoner of war. My dad made a contribution to the war effort. But he did not win the Second World War. And so the apostle says: you are part of the body, you need the church, you need other Christians because we are in it together. No matter how good a footballer you are, even if you were David Beckham (that is hard for an Evertonian like me to admit!), can you imagine taking on the Brazilian team by yourself? We know what happens when the whole England team takes on Brazil, never mind just one individual! We all need other believers.

- *How can we as a church body help each other to stay connected to Christ?*

Hold on

These regulations that were being imposed on believers often have an appearance of wisdom, 'but they lack any value in restraining sensual indulgence' (v23). There is a huge market today in the 'self-improvement' area – tapes, books, videos. You may end up looking better, feeling better, even years younger – but it is no guarantee that your heart is pure or your soul is right with God. So how do we stay connected and free? Not by petty rule keeping, that's for sure! Note verses 22 and 23. If we want to stay spiritually afloat, we must hold on to Christ.

I have had a couple of opportunities in my life to learn how to water-ski. For somebody who cannot even manage roller skates, you can imagine the problem. My first experience was in Jersey, about a decade ago. These friends had great plans for me. I was going to learn to water-ski in the English Channel. They had big speedboat and they togged me up with the rubber suit, these huge skis and a life jacket. I was trussed up like a chicken and assured it would be 'dead easy'. I had a rope with a little handle on it, and it was connected to this powerful speedboat. You just hold the handle between your bent knees and let the boat, now connected to you by the rope, take the slack and strain and then, before you know it, you are water-skiing. It's great. Fantastic! That's the theory.

I didn't know you could drink so much of the English Channel and still be alive. For the umpteenth time this thing zooms off because I had let go of the rope. I was left bobbing around like a cork in the water, trying to look cool and feeling totally stupid. My friend rolled round this big speedboat and observed me just bobbing up and down, getting very tired. He looked over the side and asked, 'Steve! Do you know what faith is?' I am thinking 'Well actually I am a Christian minister, and I could give you a dissertation on that if you − ' I simply said, 'Pardon?' He said, 'Do you know what faith is?' I said, 'Peter, tell me!' He replied, 'Faith is holding on. Do not let go of the rope!' I knew I was missing something! You can never water-ski if you let go of the rope because it isn't you, it isn't your ability. Rather, it is the power of the engine to which you are connected by a piece of rope that lifts you out the water and enables you to skim the waves. That tells us something about the nature of faith.

Russell Watson sang, at the opening ceremony of the 2002 Commonwealth Games in Manchester, that he had enough faith to reach the stars. Faith in what? What does that mean? In Scripture, it is faith's object that matters. I may have little faith in thick pack ice to support my skating on the lake. But as it could support a tank, I am safe. I may have boundless faith in some thin ice that covers our local lake, and where I intend to skate. The ice gives way, despite my great faith, and I drown by faith! If faith connects me to Christ, then I must not lose contact with him because otherwise, instead of skiing and skimming over the waves of life by the grace that connects me to his power, I will be taking in mouthfuls of salty water and feeling pretty grim and miserable. Faith in Christ, heartily trusting Jesus, is the key to freedom from bondage and fullness of life.

● *How does the picture of the motor boat and water-skiing help clarify what is your role and what is God's role in spiritual transformation?*

● *Human ways of self-improvement don't work because they 'lack any value in restraining sensual indulgence' – they cannot transform us! Share in twos an area of your life in which God has been helping you change. Pray together for an area you still need his help in.*

Further study

Verse 16 talks about not judging others on their observance of a Sabbath day. What is the view of a Sabbath day in the Old Testament and the Gospels? How does this shape your view of a Sabbath day? Is it important to keep Sunday special today?

Reflection and response

Abraham often built altars of stone to the Lord. An altar was a visual way of thanking God for the past and re-dedicating one's life to him for the future. Encourage each member of the group to bring a stone with them. This stone can symbolise the superstitions, legalism, secular rules and regulations you have been bound by. Pile the stones up together in the centre of the room. Use this act as a way to thank God for the salvation he won for us in Christ and to recommit yourselves to living in Christ's power rather than in the bondage of the past.

Review Colossians 2:1-23

Christianity isn't like the alternative spiritualities Paul has been referring to. One difference is that Christianity does not attempt to empty your mind and create a spiritual vacuum. Instead, God wants to put truth into people's minds. Christianity is a propositional religion – it can be stated and formulated. It isn't only statements of faith, but it is certainly not less. That is why verse 1:28 states, 'We proclaim him, admonishing and teaching everyone with all wisdom, so that we may present everyone perfect in Christ.'

Read through 2:1-23 again. Ask half the group to make a list of everything Christ has done for us in the past and the other half to list what our response should be to this passage.

Worship Christ for what he has done for us that we could not do ourselves. Praise God our salvation is secure!

We now need to spur each other on to live out these truths. Choose a partner with whom you can meet monthly to pray. When you meet, ask the other person if they are growing spiritually, or if they have fallen into any habits from their past. Be open and honest in return about where you are. Encourage each other with words of truth from the Bible.

Points to Ponder

- What have you learnt about God?
- What have you learnt about yourself?
- What actions or attitudes do you need to change as a result?

Chapter 10 – New directions

Aim: To grasp the new direction and focus of the Christian life

Focus on the theme

Talk together about fresh starts – when you moved house, started a new job or new church. What were the positive aspects of this change? Unfortunately, a new home or new job does not change who we are as people but a fresh start with Jesus can!

Read: Colossians 3-4:1
Key verses: Colossians 3:1-4

Heart change

Paul finishes chapter 2 by saying that human traditions and superstitions 'have an appearance of wisdom, with their self-imposed worship, their false humility and their harsh treatment of the body but they lack any value in restraining sensual indulgence.' All these petty rules and regulations seem so very clever and fantastic. They promise to help us spiritually, but actually they do nothing to tame the wild beast of lust and sinfulness that lies in every human heart. If it were not for the restraining grace of God, there is nothing that you and I could not do. Our hearts, as John Calvin put it, are 'a factory of idols.' In the human heart there is potential for great wickedness. No one is exempt – 'all have sinned and fallen short of the glory of

God' (Rom. 3:23). So ascetic practices, taboos and rituals and everything else that people use instead of Christ, actually do nothing to deal with the problem of the heart. Our hearts can only be changed and transformed by the renewing power of Jesus Christ.

As we turn to this passage, verses 1-4 will talk about setting our hearts on things above. Paul encourages us to seek those things above where Christ is seated at the right hand of God. The thought is similar in the phrase, 'set your minds on things above.' We are not to be taken up with all the taboos, superstitions and rituals of worship that were threatening the church at Colosse. Rather we have got to set our minds, affections, and hearts on Christ. All that other stuff is syncretism. That is where you take Jesus and the Christian faith and then you mix them up with something else. A missionary in Japan got a very stark illustration of that some time ago when he went into a department store at Christmas. There was a Santa Claus – crucified on a cross. That is syncretism. Father Christmas did not die for our sins!

- *Paul says 'Set your hearts on things above' (v1) and then 'Set your minds on things above' (v2). Why does he repeat the phrase using the different words 'hearts/minds'?*

- *What image comes to mind when you think of your life 'hidden with Christ in God' (v3)?*

- *Pick out the words and phrases that give you security about your salvation from v1-4.*

Get focussed

Instead of syncretism, Christians have to march to a different drumbeat: we have to run with a different rhythm to everyone else. I saw a few minutes of the Commonwealth games recently. There were two events that seemed to illustrate and strike right at the heart of what Paul is saying in these verses. Zoë Baker is a 50-metre butterfly world champion. She apparently came to the Games with two things on her mind. One, she was going to set a new world record, and she did that in the semi-finals. Two, she was going to win a gold medal in the final, which she proceeded to do. In contrast, there is a chap called Anthony Whiteman, a 1500 metre runner. He was hotly tipped to win his race. He got off to a strong start, he left it a bit late but managed to get out in front of the pack and then unbelievably he began to look around at the opposition. And then, as they came off the bend, from absolutely nowhere, another English middle distance runner appeared and won the gold medal. Where did Anthony Whiteman end up? Silver? No. Bronze? No. He just about staggered in at number 4.

What was the difference between Zoë Baker and Anthony Whiteman? Simply this: focus. She was totally focused on getting a gold and a world record. He, instead of thinking about the finishing line and forgetting the opposition, was looking round. As Seb Coe, one time world record holder said, he had a mental walkabout. He was three hundred metres from a gold medal and he forgot the whys and wherefores of running. He lost the plot. He took his eye off the goal. Now that is what Paul is saying here. If you want to make sure you win the race of Christian faith, you have got to keep remembering the goal, the finishing post. You need to set your mind on things above. For how long? This is a marathon. Christians do not finish the race till they personally die or Jesus returns. This is a daily, indeed hourly, race.

Now that said, it is important to understand what such a mindset does not mean. Some set their minds on things above as if it is things above were the only reality. So, they conclude, this world really is an illusion. But Paul isn't saying that. The rest of the chapter earths our Christianity into the hurly-burly of life in the home and the family. Nor is he saying that because this world is so evil, we should withdraw from it. Not at all. The Christian life has to be toughed out in what we call the real world. This world is a real world, since God made it, although it isn't the ultimate world.

Of course, we must not go to the other extreme. Some Christians react to all that pie-in-the-sky-when-you-die Christianity, and want to change everything here and now. They remove all the otherness of the Christian faith. They collapse heaven and all the eternal elements of faith into the here and now. So you turn up on a Sunday morning, and you hear a riveting sermon on the problems of effluent in the Rhine, or the deforestation of the Amazon, or holes in the ozone layer. It isn't that Christianity hasn't something to say about such things. It has. It is God's world. But when we focus exclusively on them, then Christianity loses its transcendence, its otherness. So people come to the church looking for a spirituality to plug the vacuum in their souls and are disappointed to find a political broadcast on animal rights but no spiritual bread to feed their spirits.

- *Give examples of what a Christian's speech or behaviour would be like if they believed this world is merely an illusion.*

- *How can your church get the right balance between being relevant to the world yet not losing its transcendence, its other worldliness? Think about this in the context of your:*

  - *Sunday morning service*
  - *Evangelistic events*
  - *Youth meetings*

Here and now: then and there

As Christians, we need to hold on to the reality of these two worlds. Some of you may know that my wife has multiple sclerosis. She was diagnosed nearly twenty-five years ago, shortly after we got married. What I have learned, in being a long-time carer (and I have to keep relearning!), is simply this: if I am going to be a wise Christian and make it through to the finishing tape with honour, I actually only need two dates in my diary. I need the date of the there and then when I will appear with Christ in glory. That is my finishing line. And I need today. The there and the then and the here and the now are the only dates, the only two polarities, between which I need to move. 'Strength for today, bright hope for tomorrow' is the deal. My great temptation in life is wanting to start crossing bridges to which I have not only not come, but which may not even exist. I need to learn the technique of setting my mind, my affections, my heart, on the finishing line.

The worst long distance run I have ever had in my life was a training run with my next-door neighbour one Saturday morning. When you run half a marathon or a marathon, at least mentally you know where you are going to finish. I had left the arrangements to this guy but it turned out he was not quite sure he knew where we were going. After seven or eight miles we were obviously lost. And so we continued to run and run and run and run. I have no idea how far we ran. It was not the longest run of my life, but certainly the worst. Why? Because nobody knew where the finishing line was. I couldn't set a pace; we were just going through the motions and thinking 'Help!' Now what sets the pace for us for this world is the next. In my today, I need to remember my tomorrow. I am going to be with Christ, I will stand before him and give an account of my time on earth. Will he be pleased or disappointed with me? That future vision gives me strength and determination to tough it out in the hurly-burly of today.

- *How does knowing 'you will appear with Christ in glory' (v4) help you make decisions and define your values today?*

- *Meditate on the phrase 'Christ, who is your life' (v4). Discuss together the richness of this phrase and how it can be more and more true of your own life.*

Reflection and response

Encourage the group to bring their diaries. We all like to be in control, and our diaries reflect how we are driven by deadlines and the pressures of this world. As you look through your diaries, reflect on that fact that only two dates really matter: today and meeting Christ in eternity. How do you need to change your priorities in the light of this? Are there any relationships you need to try to restore, anyone to whom you need to say 'sorry'?

Chapter 11 – New standards for my life

Aim: To learn to live by Christ's new standards

Focus on the theme

Discuss together how standards have varied over the last twenty years. How have living standards, fashion, and what money will buy fluctuated? Have fun looking at photos and/or receipts from the past which highlight the changes. Life brings many new things, but when Christ comes into our life he demands a change of standards, regardless of what is going on in the world.

Read: Colossians 3–4:1
Key verses: Colossians 3:5–11

Christ's life in me

In this section, Paul isn't setting down a whole new pile of rules and regulations for us, so that we tick them off. In the Old Testament, the rabbis computed that there are 613 commandments, 248 positive ones, and 365 negatives ones – a 'No' one for every day of the year! Paul isn't laying out a whole new pile of laws that Christians scrupulously have to keep. These are not so much prescriptive as descriptive; they are illustrative of what Christ's life in me means. They are moral teachings that do not go out of date. They are principles earthed in the real world, principles for Christian living, illustrating what the life of Christ in me is meant to look like.

● *What is the difference between prescriptive and descriptive? Find other contemporary and biblical examples to explain your answer.*

● *How do we know that the new standards Paul is writing about apply to us as well as to the Colossian Christians?*

An imperative starts us off: 'Put to death, therefore, whatever belongs to your earthly nature' – that means whatever belongs to your sinful heart (v5). Then he gives us a list: 'sexual immorality, impurity, lust, evil desires' – we can lump all them together, for the first word really gives the game away – 'sexual immorality.' It is the word from which we get the English word 'pornography'. In Greek porneia is often a catch-all phrase; it covers a multitude of sins. The Christian teaching on sexuality is very simple to learn, though hard to practise. For instance, the Christian faith does not teach love, sex and marriage. It teaches love, marriage, and sex. In that order – period! Scripture condemns any form of sexual activity outside the bonds of marriage.

You notice the passage says, it is because of such things 'the wrath of God is coming' (v6). God will hold me to account one day. In this area of sexuality, here is what the Christ-life looks like – it is walking with God, it is seeking for a pure heart. The way you view and treat other people, whether of the same or opposite sex, and of whatever age, is to be with absolute purity. It is at this point, of course, that many Christians want to start putting all sorts of rules and regulations in place. How long should a woman's skirts or a man's hair be? What should or shouldn't you wear on a beach, plus a whole pile of taboos and regulations. But the heart of the principle isn't whether you wear lipstick or make-up. The issue is being godly, sexually pure and faithful.

Moreover, it is very easy to mistake cultural norms for the principle. When my good friend Alistair Begg was a young lad, his Sunday school would take their annual 'treats' on the waters of the River Clyde. On one occasion in the early 1960s, he heard a group of men in animated discussion. They were really getting worked up, and Alistair, being Alistair, listened in on their debate. He kept hearing, 'pertaineth, pertaineth, pertaineth – the woman shall not wear that which pertaineth to the man.' It is a verse found at Deuteronomy 22:5. Then he cottoned on – a lady had turned up for this Sunday School outing on a Saturday morning, wearing a pair of slacks. 'The woman shall not wear that which pertaineth to the man.' How dare she! But the irony of the situation was that the men were all wearing kilts!

When it comes to this area of sexual purity, it is about making wise decisions and choices. I remember a young guy, who, before he was a Christian, had slept with more women than he could remember. He had had a number of children by different partners. He would come and tell me how he had visited one of his children and one of his ex-partners, the mother of the child. Somehow one thing had led to another, and he had fallen into sin – he had slept with the woman again. This went on for some time until eventually I said to him, 'Harry, I have heard enough of this. You don't just end up in bed with someone. This does not just happen, you have made a thousand other decisions before you get to that point.' Bless him, he took it on the chin and made the necessary adjustments.

If you are a wise Christian, you are going to need to take evasive action. You need to take the right decisions before temptation gets too strong. Some of us guys, particularly when we go away from home, need to be very careful, don't we? There are TV channels and programmes that would make our grannies blush and our wives ashamed. I belong to the Association of Bible College Principals, a body that represents over half of those studying theology in the UK at undergraduate level today. Another college principal was telling me that when his college offered free internet access to all their students, more than one student came to him and said, 'Please don't do it. We have too much temptation already.' Let him who has ears to hear, hear!

- *Guiding children and teenagers through the moral maze is notoriously difficult. Use the following scenarios to discuss how we can teach our young people the biblical principles of sexual morality rather than being influenced by the cultural norms:*

  - *You have found out a couple in the youth group are sleeping together. What do you do?*
  - *Your fifteen year old daughter wants to go to a mixed sleepover with school friends. How do you respond?*
  - *Your teenage son has a computer in his room to do his homework. How do you protect his viewing and yet teach him responsibility?*

The list continues – covetousness, greed, unchecked desires for pleasure, money 'which is idolatry' (v5). For instance, Scripture says 'six days shalt thou labour.' Some of us know better than God. I know all the difficulties of the market-place and demands on many employees. But you have got to make sure you get time for God. Is that extra holiday that you worked so hard for, hardly seeing your children in the process, really worthwhile? Are you sure it is God-honouring? Are you able to rearrange your life and your lifestyle to reflect God's priorities rather than just having more money in the bank, a bigger house or a newer car?

Then we have the more decent sins, as many would see them, 'You used to walk in these ways ... now you must rid yourselves of all such things as these: anger, rage, malice, slander and filthy language from your lips' (v8). Some folk are always on a short fuse, aren't they? Christians, as well. A Californian minister one morning was going off to speak at a prayer break-fast. He was really wound up about it. He was always on a short fuse, always living on the edge. He was actually going to be speaking at a prayer breakfast where a senator would be. So he was really pleased with himself. When he got to his car, he noticed it had a flat tyre, so he quickly changed the wheel. Oops! Now he had a tyre mark on his off-white suit. He went back indoors, changed, and then he noticed he had cut himself shaving earlier. The blood had dripped onto his shirt, so then he had to change that. By now he was really running late. He jumped into his car and was zooming along the highway when, out of nowhere, came one of those Chips bikes. The Californian Highway Patrol man pulled him over. He lets the window down and says, 'Just give me the ticket, officer, just give me the ticket! I was really going so fast, I was probably going even faster than you could even imagine, so just give me that ticket, I am really in a rush!' The officer said, 'Cool down, sir, take it easy.' He said, 'No, no, you don't understand. Give me that ticket. Give me that ticket now, I confess it!' The officer said, 'Look, calm down, sir, calm down.' He said, 'No, you don't understand, I have got a really important meeting I have to get to.' The patrol officer persisted, 'Sir, calm down.' 'No, no, no!' 'Sir,' he said, 'Can I just give you a piece of advice? I used to have days like you, but three months ago I became a Christian'!

● *Is there any biblical evidence that God has gradations of sin, where some sins are less serious than others?*

The power of words

People say, 'Words don't matter.' Jesus said something different. He said by our words we will be justified or condemned. Words can help or heal, they can hurt or hinder, they can bless or destroy. When I was six years old, I had a schoolteacher called

Miss Evans. I guess I was misbehaving in class. And she had a cure for miscreants like me. I can still hear her voice, 'Stephen Brady, come and put your ugly face into the corner at the front of the class!' I went home to my mum and told her 'Miss Evans told me to put my ugly face into the corner.' Everybody needs a mum like mine! She went down to that school faster than an Exocet missile. HMS Edie Brady! I tell you, I don't think Miss Evans has said an unkind word to anybody ever since! More seriously, some of us have gone through life carrying all sorts of painful baggage because somebody said something unkind to us and we did not have a Mum to fight our corner. There is an incredible power in words. God has given us the gift of language but before we speak, we need to **think** about what we are about to say – is it **T**rue, is it **H**elpful, is it **I**mportant, is it **N**ecessary, is it **K**ind? If it isn't, then don't say it!

- *Look up other verses in the Bible that remind us to use our tongues wisely – for example, Proverbs 10:11, 16:23-24; Matthew 12:34-37, 15:18-20; James 1:26, 3:3-12.*

Paul continues, 'Do not lie to each other, since you have taken off your old self with its practices and you have put on the new self, which is being renewed in the knowledge of its Creator' (v9-10). What is the picture here? Paul is working with two 'bookends' in his mind when it comes to people. These two bookends are the first Adam and the last Adam, Christ. Hence, in 1 Corinthians 15 or Romans 5, he talks about being 'in Adam' or being 'in Christ.' A Christian is someone who is no longer just 'in Adam', the old self, who is sinful and wayward and in rebellion towards God. By the grace of God, they are now 'in Christ.' Paul isn't just giving us a text for self-improvement here. He is saying, 'God has done something radical for you in Christ – Christ died so he might take you out of the old humanity and put you into the new.' Through Adam all humanity dies. But to be in Christ, that is life. Indeed, to be like Jesus is to be truly human, for the only perfect human being ever seen on planet earth since the fall of Adam is Christ.

When I was a little lad, my Dad was a bus driver in my native Liverpool. Every so often he would get a new bus to try out. They were named E1, E2, E3 etc, prototypes of a potential new fleet of buses. Occasionally, I used to meet him at a pre-arranged time, and along would come the bus, on it I would go, and sit there proud as punch thinking, 'My Dad's driving this bus!' The Chief Engineer and his team at Edge Lane Works, Liverpool, would make a decision about which prototype would be used for the new fleet. Before long, tens then hundreds of new buses – Leyland Atlanteans, I recall – would be zipping round Liverpool. All because somebody had decided that this prototype was precisely the kind of bus Liverpool City Transport needed. Now God has decided what humanity's shape is going to be. For that he has a prototype – Christ. Not the 'old Adam' – sinful, selfish, wayward. Rather, the new One – God-centred, obedient, good. Therefore, to be in Christ is to become authentically human and increasingly human. Accordingly, when we are in Christ, we must not forget who we are.

Verse 11 reminds us, 'Here there is no Greek or Jew, circumcised or uncircumcised, barbarian, Scythian, slave or free, but Christ is all, and is in all.' Therefore, we do not judge people by their background, their intelligence, their social class or the colour of their skin. Paul is saying there are only two kinds of people – those who are in the old Adam and those in the new Adam; those in Christ and those without him. That is what makes all the difference, in this world and the next.

- *When exactly did we 'take off the old self' and 'put on the new self' (v 9-10)?*

- *If we have already 'put on the new self' why do we still have a sinful 'earthly nature' (v5)? Explain the decisive transaction that* happened when we became Christians and the part that is an ongoing process.

- *How can we help ourselves keep God's new standards? Share practical examples of how we can 'put to death our earthly nature' (v5) and facilitate our new self 'being renewed in knowledge in the image of its Creator' (v10).*

Reflection and response

To what extent are you living by God's standards? In what specific areas are you still allowing your 'earthly nature' to dominate? The hard truth is that when we live like we did in the past, we are denying the power and reality of our salvation. We are saying that to us Christ's death counts for nothing. Pray in twos about one sin you are going to 'put to death' this week. Pray throughout the week that in that particular area you will each live up to God's new standard.

Chapter 12 – New standards for the church

Aim: To live out God's new standards in the church community

Focus on the theme

Brainstorm together the standards you have for your small group – what values and activities are important to you? How does your list of standards compare with the list God gives in these verses?

Read: Colossians 3–4:1
Key verses: Colossians 3:12–4:1

Virtues

Compassion
In verse 12 Paul gives the Christian church, Christian believers, titles that were used of the Old Testament people of God – you are God's chosen people, you are holy, you are dearly loved. Then he speaks about our attitude in the light of that. Sin, as we have seen earlier, brings only fragmentation and disintegration. What damage our temper, our tongue and our lust can do! Instead, here are virtues that bring integration into life, wholeness to our personality. The virtue he starts with is 'compassion.' It is a word used of Jesus when he saw the crowds (Mt. 9:36). It is a strong word. It means 'moved to the very core of your

being' with concern. Christianity is a religion of compassion, of kindness. The early church was noted for its kindness to all sorts of people on the edges of society. The church has a brilliant record for its inspirational care for the disadvantaged, the blind, the orphan and the poor. It is easy to knock the church. Has any other society on earth – with all its failures granted – such a track record?

- *Why is it significant that Paul chooses titles used of the children of Israel to refer to these New Testament believers in verse 12? What relevance is this to us?*

- *How do we 'clothe ourselves' (v12) with these Christian virtues?*

Gentleness

Then there is gentleness. It could be translated 'meekness.' That is what Jesus spoke of when he said, 'Blessed are the meek, they will inherit the earth.' But what is meekness? Weakness? Meekness is like being at a set of traffic lights in your new top of the range Porsche that is capable of reaching sixty mph, from a standing start, in under four seconds. Next to you is a guy in a Robin Reliant. And he is revving his engine, preparing for the chariot race. He is looking at you, and as soon as the amber light comes on he is away, flat out. What is meekness? Putting your foot down and saying 'See ya!'? No, meekness is letting him do it when you could burn him off the road, and he would only see your slip stream. Meekness is strength and power under control – you don't cut people down to size just because you are bigger and smarter than they are.

Next comes patience, long-suffering; the long fuse, not the short temper. We say of some people that they 'do not suffer fools gladly.' Some folk don't appear to suffer anyone at all. But here is the quality of suffering fools and everyone else gladly for Jesus' sake. After all, he suffers us! His patience and long-suffering are the reason why we are still here. Likewise, we are mandated to exercise restraint, to be truly cool, even in the face of extreme provocation.

Forgiveness

Next, we are to 'forgive as the Lord forgave you, and over all these virtues put on love, which binds them all together' (v13-14). Forgiveness in verse 13 literally means 'to grace' – as God has 'graced' you, 'grace' others. This theme of forgiveness is central to the Christian faith, of course. In Christ's death, God has gone to the ultimate length to forgive us so we can go free. But I know, from many years as a pastor, about the troubled lives of people who will not forgive, not let go and move on. They certainly damage the people around them. But there is often incredible damage, initially unseen, that they do to themselves as well. Some of us need to forgive our children. Some of us need to forgive our parents. Some of us need to forgive that person who broke our heart and wrecked our lives, maybe all those years ago, and towards whom we still feel so bitter. You say, 'But you don't know what she did to me!' No, I don't. But I know what your sins and mine did to Christ, so we could go free. While you hold on to that bitterness you are not going to walk and make progress with Christ. So 'over all these things put on love' (v14). Put on the love that is patient and kind, not jealous or boastful, not arrogant or rude, the love that is the love of Christ.

- *If all Christians pursue these virtues, are we in danger of becoming clones and losing the distinctive personalities God gave us?*

- *Love for the saints was evidence (1:4) that the Colossians were truly saved. Now in 3:14 they are told to 'put on love.' Explain the tension between the Holy Spirit's work in our lives and the effort we need to exert to be Christ-like.*

The peace of Christ

Next, Paul speaks specifically to the church in verses 15-17. The 'you and your' in these verses are plural. He says 'Let the peace of Christ rule in your hearts.' Of course, we can individually know the peace of God, but here is a church full of peacefulness. We live in a warring, hurting, dysfunctional world. The local church is meant to be an oasis of peace and healing for damaged people and communities. Bill Hybels of Willow Creek Community Church, USA, is right: 'The local church is the hope of the world.' The assumption, of course, in that statement is that the particular local church is a place where the Lord Jesus is truly central. Then the local church isn't merely happy but healthy, functioning as she should – salt and light in her community (Mt. 5:13-16). The alternative is tragic – when such a church is no different from the world outside – fighting, gossiping, cold-shouldering each other, playing power games and having turf wars about who does what. Peace and unity in the local church are to be highly prized and carefully guarded. As someone has wisely remarked, 'The world at its worst needs the church at its best.'

In addition to being a peaceful church, a local church needs to be a biblical one; as verse 16 says, 'let the word of Christ dwell in you richly.' The word of God is central to the well-being of the church. The Bible is ignored to our peril. Yet in many churches today, Scripture is marginalized and Bible teaching neglected. Moreover, this is a worshipping church, utilising psalms, hymns and spiritual songs. Some churches just sing the psalms. Others only enjoy good old hymns – especially if they were written before the twentieth century. Other churches use only spiritual songs. There are other ways of understanding these three categories and how they apply to public worship. But it seems to me to be the path of wisdom, in our specific worship services, to have a blend of psalms, hymns and spiritual songs. 'What God hath joined together, let

no man put asunder'! Let's be wisely eclectic, flexible yet testing everything by Scripture, so that whatever 'we do, whether
in word or deed, do it all in the name of the Lord Jesus, giving
thanks to God the Father through him' (v17).

- *On a scale of 1-10 (1 being poor and 10 being excellent), how
  would you rate your church in the qualities that Paul
  advocates:*

  - *Peacefulness (v15)*
  - *Thankfulness (v15)*
  - *Word-centredness v16 – look for evidence not just in the ser-
    mon but in the way you relate to each other (v16), and in the
    content as well as the music used in worship (v17)*

- *What can you as an individual do to improve the situation?*

- *Using verses 16-17 as a starting point, what criteria do you think
  we should use to choose the musical items for our church
  services?*

Marriage

In verses 18-19 Paul addresses married people. Some of us who
read these verses are single, widowed or divorced. However, we
ought not to think we can simply skip this section. We all need
to uphold the sanctity of marriage. On the other hand, married
people need to be far more sensitive and aware of the singles
around them – and ensure they are always included in the
church family and not only for baby-sitting services! Nor
should singles be the butt of insensitive comments – 'and when
are you going to find a nice young man, then?'… 'your
husband's been gone now all of six months – time you were
over it, you know, life must go on!'

If we are married, however, then this passage speaks specifically to us. Let us begin by looking at this word 'submit.' There are different ways of expressing ourselves with language. For example, 'I hit' is what we call active. 'I am hit', is passive. But when 'I hit myself', that is called reflexive, or what in Greek is known as the middle voice. Now the word 'submit' here is in the middle voice. Submitting to her husband is what the woman does herself, it is something that she willingly and deliberately does. This isn't a question of female inferiority. That isn't the issue at all. Scripture makes it abundantly clear that both by creation (Gen. 1:27,28) and new creation in Christ (Gal. 3:28), men and women are equal in the sight of God. Rather, it is a matter of how things operate in the home. Here is a first century woman, who is living in a social context where she had very few if any legal rights and where the husband's word was law. Yet remarkably Paul says she actually has something she can do, she has a choice about this; she can learn to submit to her husband willingly, as is fitting in the Lord, as it is appropriate to her culture. Indeed, one of the root meanings of submit has the idea of order! She finds God's order for her own life, domestically and otherwise.

Let's fast forward to our century where, in the western world especially, we are deeply impacted by what is known as feminism. Let it be said immediately that this movement has brought some very real gains to many women who have been the victims of abusive and violent husbands or of gross injustices in the workplace. In a culture such as we find in the UK, to suggest a woman should submit even to her husband is the proverbial red rag to a bull. On the other hand, if part of the idea of submitting is finding order, isn't order in our homes – and God's order in particular – desirable? Have you ever had the experience of visiting a home where a woman is constantly undermining her husband, 'Take no notice of him, he doesn't know anything, speak to me'? Or a man speaking about his wife, 'I make sure she dresses in white to colour-match all the other kitchen appliances'? She has assumed the role of the domineering female, he of the male chauvinist. The Bible says such attitudes are not appropriate.

What is the answer to the domineering male or the under-mining female with her insulting put-downs? Open season? Hardly! Husbands, for instance, are told in verse 19 to 'love your wives and don't be harsh with them.' The word 'harsh' suggests a couple of ideas. Firstly, do not be either physically or verbally violent in any way with your wife. Husbands, you are to love your wife as Christ loved the church (see Eph. 5:25). Secondly, do not become embittered when your wife does not come up to scratch, when she isn't always submissive to you, when she gives you back as good as you are giving her! Husbands, at that point, do not head for your cave, sulk and become hard and bit-ter. And wives – don't wait to get even! Lighten up – love her. Husbands and wives, let the gospel re-order your marriage and home.

Parents and children

Verses 20-21 say 'Children, obey your parents in everything … Fathers, do not embitter your children.' Do you notice how reciprocal these two verses are? 'Fathers, do not embitter your children.' You can do that in so many ways. One sure-fire method is to have family favourites. Read all about it in Genesis 27, and the years of pain and division it caused in Isaac and Rebekah's home for their twin boys, Esau and Jacob. And children are to obey! That is a process to be taught. It takes time and patience to 'bend the will without breaking the spirit', as Dr James Dobson of *Focus on the Family* puts it. There are times when your children can drive you to the edge. Yet they need boundaries.

One mum had just got to the end of her tether with her eight year old boy. He knew he was in trouble when she said,

'Come here!' So, he flew upstairs, as he often did, and he crawled under the big double bed and got right in the corner, out of the way reach of his dear old Mum. She threatened him: 'You wait till your father gets home!' When Dad came home, Mum said, 'He has been so naughty today. Now he is up there, under the bed, I cannot reach him or get him out!' Dad went upstairs, got down on the floor near the bed and started to get underneath it when the little boy said, 'Dad, is she after you as well? I'll move over!'

Workplace

What about the workplace? In the sixties, I used to work in local government. I had just become a Christian and I tried my best to feel enthusiastic. Yawn! Then I discovered verse 23, 'whatever you do, work at it with all your heart, as working for the Lord, not men.' That revolutionised my life and thinking as a local government officer. I could do my daily job for Jesus. Nothing is too small, humble or insignificant if done for Christ. Remember, in the first instance, these words were spoken to slaves who had no legal rights, no employment legislation to protect them, no union shop steward in their corner.

On the other side of the coin, isn't it shocking when you employ a Christian to do a job for you, perhaps a plumber, mechanic, builder or lawyer, and he is a shoddy workman? He may say, 'Nice to have had fellowship with you,' as he leaves you with that big bill, still singing his choruses on the way out to his pick-up truck. But you know the heating isn't working or the roof still leaks.

If you are a Christian in the market place, whether you are in bonds or boilers, you need to do it for Christ. That is to be the emphasis, that is to be your motivation. We need the Christ-life to show itself in the workplace. That does not mean ramming religion down people's throats. It will mean talking the talk, of course. But it will only count as you walk the talk. It can be so tough in the workplace today – dog eat dog. Christians ought to march to a different drumbeat – the beat of God's gracious heart. And if you are an employer, provide for your employees 'what is right and fair, because you know you have a Master in heaven to whom we are all accountable' (4:1, and see 2 Cor. 5:10). After all, 'the worker deserves his wages', according to Jesus (Lk. 10:7).

- *In 3:18-4:1 pick out the words, phrases and ideas which indicate that knowing Christ gives value to marginalized groups in society – for the Colossians this was women, children and slaves.*

What is the secret to this whole new way of life? It is mentioned for us three times. Verse 1 reminds us that we were 'raised with Christ' in the past; verse 3, in the present, my life is 'hidden with Christ'; and verse 4, in the future I 'will appear with Christ' in glory. Mohammad Ali was taking a plane journey while he was still heavyweight champion of the world. The stewardess came along and said, 'Mr Ali, would you please fasten your seatbelt?' He looked at her and said, 'Superman don't need no seatbelt.' She looked at him and replied, 'Superman don't need no plane. Fasten your belt!' As we look at these qualities, we may easily think, 'Do I have to be Superman, Superwoman?' No, you don't. Christ is the secret – it is being 'with Christ.' It is getting on board Christ. Having a relationship with Christ means that in our workplaces, marriages, family lives and churches, the life of Jesus by the Holy Spirit is so coursing through our veins, that in all things Jesus has the pre-eminence in that daily event we call life.

- *How can we have a deeper experience of life with Christ? At what points or under what circumstances has your experience of life with Christ been deeper than it is now?*

Further study

Submission is almost a politically incorrect word in our culture. How does the context of this verse help us understand how Paul wants us to interpret the term? Look at what Paul says to all Christians and what he says to husbands in particular in 3:1-4:1.

Reflection and response

No one can live their Christian life in isolation. We were designed to live as Christians in community – in the context of family, church and work. We are to help each other clothe ourselves in the Christ-like virtues. Try using a visual aid to remind you: as you leave, exchange your jacket or overcoat with someone – or if that isn't practical, swap gloves, scarves, ties or watches. As you wear someone else's possession for a week, let it remind you to put on love like an overcoat on top of all the other Christian virtues (v14).

Review Colossians 3:1-4:1

The key to living the Christian life is to focus on Christ – remembering all that he has done for us, meditating on what he has made us and living in the light of it. This means relinquishing habits and attitudes from our old way of life and living to please him. We do not just please God by doing religious things. Rather, we please him in everyday life in the family, at work and at church as we do things the way he would if he were here.

● *Trace the use of the words God, Lord, and Christ in chapter 3. What impression do you get? How could you make your life more God/Christ-focused? Think through these key areas and perhaps talk about them with a friend:*

- *What personally do I have to deal with to become more like Christ – what do I have to do/stop doing?*

- *How could I make my church and the ministry I am involved in more Christ-centred?*

- *How could I make my marriage more God-honouring?*

- *What changes could I bring to our family life to make Christ more of a priority?*

- *How could I change my attitude and behaviour at work to serve Christ rather than just my boss?*

Points to Ponder

- *What have you learnt about God?*
- *What have you learnt about yourself?*
- *What actions or attitudes do you need to change as a result?*

Chapter 13 – Persevering in prayer

Aim: To have a strong and committed prayer life

Focus on the theme

Share together a time when you experienced close fellowship with God in prayer or a really memorable prayer meeting. Why were those times special? What made them significant for you?

Read: Colossians 4:2–18
Key verses: Colossians 4:2–4

Keep going

The well-known, well-travelled Argentinean evangelist Luis Palau, some years ago now, was asked what was his cardinal temptation as a Christian worker. Money? Sex? Pride? He replied, 'None of those things. My major temptation is to want to give up sometimes.' If we are not careful in life, we may end up living in another place just north of Keswick, a place called 'Weary Hall'! Have you grown tired of well-doing, and taken up residence in Weary Hall and yet are miserable there? You need a move! Have you felt like giving up lately? That isn't unusual. Paul knew this, so in the early chapters of this letter he has reminded us of the foundational truths: Christ has died for us, Christ is risen for us, Christ is our life, Christ is at the Father's right hand where he intercedes for us, and he will come again. In the light of Christ, Paul now spells out for us the ethical implications of what it means to be a Christian in a tough and a difficult world.

● *What do you find most difficult about being a Christian?*

● *Have you found prayer to be a help or a hindrance when you are facing these difficulties?*

How do we press on? Firstly, we need to be prayerful (v2-3). Paul started his letter with a great prayer (see 1:3-8). Here he returns to this topic, wanting to enlist these Colossian believers as his fellow prayer warriors. 'Devote yourselves to prayer, being watchful and thankful.' It is so encouraging when people pray for you, isn't it; when people take you to their hearts. I remember, over twenty years ago now, speaking at the old Filey Convention, organised by the Movement for World Evangel-isation. A few years later, in the mid-80s, I was on holiday in North Wales. An older lady tapped me on the shoulder. 'Excuse me, are you Stephen Brady? she asked in a rich Welsh accent. 'Yes', I replied.' 'Oh,' she said, 'God laid you on my heart at Filey, and I pray for you and your dear family every day.' I had never met this lady, Peggy, before but her words were such an encour-aging and a humbling experience for me.

● *Colossians 4:12 tells us Epaphras prayed for the church members as well as Paul. What one person are you praying specif-ically for?*

Keep praying

What does he want these Colossian believers to do? First, to be faithful in prayer. Devote yourselves to prayer, be staunch about it, persevere in it. 'Pray without ceasing' says

1 Thessalonians 5:17. In other words, this is something that is essential for us as Christians. Stay constantly in touch with God throughout the day. Be like Nehemiah when he came before Artaxerxes in Nehemiah 2. He tells us, 'I prayed to the God of heaven, and I said to the king...' An arrow prayer. A fax request. An email to God. It is like breathing – stop and you die. 'The Christian's vital breath', we used to call prayer. Moment by moment, we need to keep in touch with God. You don't need to bow your head and close your eyes when you pray. For some of us, if we do that, the temptation is to fall asleep! But we do need to be alert.

'Be watchful' – stay awake, stay alert. Why should I be watchful? Because I need to be watchful for answers to prayer, that's for sure. I need to be watchful for the Lord is coming, that is an ultimate certainty. But I also need to be watchful because Jesus tells us to watch and pray lest we enter into temptation (Mt. 26:41). 'Seven days without prayer', as the old saying goes, 'makes one weak.' We are not to allow our prayer life to become dull, lifeless and listless. Instead, there has to be a passion and an energy about our praying.

Look at Nehemiah again, this time chapter 1. There is a delightful phrase, 'I beseech.' That is real praying. In the Hebrew it is one word, a word that a servant would use to get something from his master – a begging word. You really mean it! If God does not show up you have nowhere else to go! The Lord wants us to pray with a fervency and expectancy like that. In addition, we need lots of thankfulness mingled with our prayers – an attitude of gratitude. We need to learn to be thankful, to count our blessings! We grieve the Holy Spirit when we are critical! There are people I know who are totally abstainers when it comes to alcohol. But they have a whine cellar that intoxicates them and those around them with bitterness. There is nothing like gratitude to God to develop a Christlike, sweet spirit within us – 'give thanks in all circumstances' (1 Thes. 5:18). Be thankful.

- *Past generations seem to have been more devoted to prayer than we are today:*

  - *Why do think this is the case?*
  - *How can devotion to prayer be more incorporated into your life?*

- *What does it mean to be 'watchful in prayer' (v2)?*

Pray specifically

We are to be prayerful generally, thankful always and purposeful in our prayers. Verse 3 says 'pray for us, too, that God may open a door for our message, so that we may proclaim the mystery of Christ.' What is Paul's request here? Note that he does not ask them to pray along these lines: 'You know I am in prison. Would you pray that the prison doors would fling open like they have before (Acts 16:26)? Then I will be able to walk free from this Roman prison and maybe Caesar will be converted because he will hear that an angel did it.' No, Paul asks for an open door, not out of prison but for the gospel. 'Pray for me', he says, so that he might proclaim the mystery of Christ, for which he had been imprisoned.

This is what I would call the difference between shotgun and rifle praying. Do you know what I mean? Rifles take bullets and when you fire a bullet, you just have one target. Shotguns, on the other hand, use buckshot and the further it travels, the more it sprays everywhere. It is only generally effective. Paul is saying, 'I don't just want you generally to fire at heaven with buckshot. I want you to pray specifically.' We have all heard prayers like 'Lord, please bless all the missionaries and all the doctors in all the world everywhere all the time and especially today.' But what do you want God to do? How can you be watchful for an answer to prayer if you pray that generally? It isn't wrong to pray generally (1 Tim. 2:1-2). But Paul's specific request is that when he opens his mouth he might be able to proclaim the gospel clearly.

● *Paul is asking people he never met to pray for him. This can be very difficult. Share together any helpful ideas about how to pray for missionaries and others whom you have only heard about or see occasionally.*

Yes but how?

When I hear some preachers, I can be deeply challenged in all sorts of ways. But I am always looking for what is called the 'YBH Factor.' I know I need to read my Bible more. I know I should give more. I know I should pray more. I know I should evangelise more. I know I should do this and that and the other – Yes, But How? We all know that we should eat, unless we are fasting or planning to die. Most of us know it is a good idea to have a good night's sleep regularly. It is beneficial in all sorts of ways beyond the pay cheque to hold down a job or to write that essay, clean the house, and a whole host of other things too. How do we get round to doing such things? Simple – you plan it! You set certain times aside to do these things.

Some people say, 'We don't want to get into all that legalistic nonsense of quiet times.' If that is you, then I need to let you know that you have a major theological problem! It isn't, biblically speaking, legalism to read your Bible, to say your prayers, to walk with God, to meet with God's people and build yourself up in your faith. If you think that is legalism, you have misunderstood the gospel. Legalism is when you think those things are going to get you to heaven. On the other hand, discipleship inevitably means I am going to be disciplined. So I need to work out times when I can meet with God. They may have to be flexible. We have got to find out how we are personally wired up – some of us may be morning people, others are night owls. I am much more alert at 1am than 1pm. I find my most creative times and my most concentrated times of prayer are not early morning but later in the day. The last morning I woke up feeling great was August 1966 – write to me for details as to the why! Other people wake up with a bang, all the lights are on and they are firing away on all cylinders. So for them that is a great time to pray. Know how you tick. When you do, make sure you plan some of your best time to pray.

When I was a pastor of a church in Bournemouth, we had a network of some seven hundred adults, plus loads of children and young people. I felt it part of my pastoral responsibility to pray regularly for those members and friends of the congregation. I could not pray for everybody every day in detail. I used a list of the people so that, over the course of a month, I could plan to pray for each of them by name. Now I still find that such lists help me – whether it is praying for other Christian workers or family and friends. The great danger, of course, is you can just run through the names and not really enter into it. That is a problem, I know, but it isn't legalism. I am just trying to be wise in how I pray and taking time to plan it.

Do you find praying hard? Here is something else that is practical. Notice that all the verbs Paul uses are in the plural. Of course, he assumes personal prayer. But isn't it often so much easier to pray with one or two others? 'Two and threes' are Jesus type numbers, remember – (see Mt. 18:19 and 20). Think of it by way of an analogy. I am a keen jogger. For a number of years, I arranged for one or more joggers to be on my doorstep early morning to jog together – I have already mentioned I am not a morning person! Without these guys, when I wake up, I don't feel like jogging, I am too tired, I make excuses. But knowing that bell is going to ring and will wake the whole household kicks me out of bed. Just as it is often much easier to jog with others, so it is often easier to pray with a small group. There are times for personal prayer, but there are also times and occasions when praying with friends, family or a partner is vital.

- *At times it is difficult to know what to pray for people. Look at some of Paul's other prayers and draw up a list of the main thing he prays for people. Look at 2 Thessalonians 1:11-12, Philemon 6, Philippians 1:9-10, Ephesians 3:16-19.*

- *Discuss practices that you have found useful to keep your own prayer life fresh and consistent.*

- *Spend some time in prayer. Use your answers to question 7 to pray specifically for:*

  - *Your church leaders and gospel preachers.*
  - *Your church ministries.*
  - *Special evangelistic events like* Alpha *or* Christianity Explored.

Further study

- *In 4:2 Paul mentions again the importance of being thankful. Trace the idea of thankfulness through the book of Colossians. What is Paul thankful for? What should we be thankful for?*
- *If your church does not have a list of people who attend and the ministries your church runs, think about compiling one so that people can pray more effectively.*

Reflection and response

Even in his difficult circumstances, Paul prayed for an opening for the gospel (v3). Could you use your present difficulties as an opportunity to start praying for an opening to share the gospel? Notice too that at least part of Paul's gifting as an evangelist was down to the prayers of believers like the Colossians (v4). Who in Christian ministry could you be praying for regularly?

Chapter 14 – Evangelism

Aim: To be resourceful in our evangelism

Focus on the theme

*Describe to each other the really good personal evangelists you know.
What do you admire about them? How do they challenge you? This
exercise may help you think through how sharing the gospel can become
a regular part of your own life.*

Read: Colossians 4:2-18
Key verses: Colossians 4:5-6

The God stuff

Remember Paul is in prison. Philippians 1:12-14, 4:22 give us a
clue as to what actually happened whilst he was in chains. All the
time, four Roman soldiers would have guarded him. Every few
hours the guard would change. You can imagine Paul turning
the conversation to the gospel. He had a captive audience – the
guards couldn't go anywhere since they were looking after him,
and he was going nowhere! So he says, verse 4, 'pray that I may
proclaim it (the gospel) clearly, as I should.' Paul knows that just
sharing the gospel without prayer counts for nothing. I think it
is Bill Hybels who talks about the God stuff happening when
you preach or share the gospel. By that he means the Lord turning up and doing what he alone can do – giving spiritual sight
and hearing and life! This isn't an automatic, slot machine

religion. Prayer reminds us of our utter dependence on God. Just recently, a colleague on the staff at Moorlands College told me of an evangelistic strategy he and others developed for their town. It was brilliant! The mission week arrived – this could not fail. The only person who did not turn up was God. The result – no one was converted. As Paul shares the gospel he is praying that the God stuff would happen. We know from Philippians that the result was that people in Caesar's household were converted through this captive evangelist.

- *Write down on a large sheet of paper what you understand to be the fundamental elements of the gospel message.*

In contrast to my last illustration, I had the privilege, a little while ago, of visiting a church in Northern Ireland that pulls in about three thousand people each Sunday evening. Every Sunday they have decisions for Christ. If you ask the pastor what is the secret of his church's growth, he will tell you it is an open secret! The church draws between eight and nine hundred every week to its prayer meeting. They pray for him and they pray that the gospel will go out in power. Prayer and evangelism, prayer and world mission, are inextricably linked. As an old Puritan put it, 'When God intends great blessing for his people, he sets them a-praying.' Alongside *Alpha* and *Christianity Explored* and every other means of evangelism, we will only be used if we pray. Then we continue to witness for Jesus, wherever God has placed us.

Think of some of these locations. Some of us are in not-yet-Christian homes. I came to faith from a non-church-going background like that. It sure keeps you on your toes when you are the only committed Christian in the home! Many of us are in the workplace. Some of us are in education. Others of us have young families. So, we meet other mums at mums and toddlers groups or at the school gate. Some of us live in retirement homes, and may be tempted to think the Lord has put us out to grass. But there is no grass where we are because it isn't a field we are in but an airport departure lounge! Flights are being called all the time. The Lord has placed you there to remind your fellow residents or passengers to ensure that Jesus is on board when their flight is called. Then they will be on the right plane for the right destination. Wherever God has placed us, there we are called to be witnesses for Christ.

Do we need qualifications, such as a degree from a Bible college like mine at Moorlands to be an effective witness? That can help! But most of us will not have that opportunity or privilege. Rather, there are the non-negotiables we need to be an effective witness for Jesus. First, live with integrity – 'Be wise in the way you act towards outsiders' (v5). Literally, Paul wrote, 'Walk in wisdom.' That word walk picks up all the teaching he has already given back in chapter 3. How are Christians to live? By putting some things off – immorality, misbehaviour etc – and putting some things on – compassion, mercy and becoming like Christ. If we are going to be good witnesses for Jesus, it isn't only what we say, but also the integrity of our lives that counts. We are to walk, to live out, the Christian life, to be consistent specifically for the sake of outsiders.

The out-crowd

Who are the outsiders? Let us take a clue from Mark's gospel. Mark talks often about the crowd. But they are not the in-crowd, those close to Jesus. They are outsiders. Interestingly, the Bible never talks about those outsiders as the unsaved. They are not unsaved as far as the Bible is concerned. There is another word – lost. They are 'like sheep without a shepherd' (Mt. 9:36). They don't know that the Shepherd has left the ninety-nine to come to seek and to save them, and that he longs to put them on his shoulder and to bring them home rejoicing (Lk. 15:1-8). They are lost in their sins and don't know it. The result is they are wrapped up in themselves, in their self-sufficiency, their careers, their education, their families, their pleasures, believing that only this world matters. The call is to walk in wisdom so that Christians are a good advert for these folks, signposts to an altogether different world and value system. Here is the reminder of the vital importance of solid Christian character, men and women whose lives back up what we say.

I heard a story of a man who was preaching in a church in his home town one evening. He had preached about being a Christian and walking with God. He gave a good evangelistic address. The next morning, he got on a bus to go to work. He gave a pound coin to the driver, for a 60p fare. However, the driver gave him 60p change, not 40p. Just before his stop, he went back to the driver, 'Excuse me, you gave me too much change. You should have given me 40p and you gave me 60p.' The driver looked at him and said, 'I know. I heard you speak last night and I just wanted to make sure that your Christianity made a difference on a Monday morning.' What a challenge to live with integrity!

- *Brainstorm the five key things you think outsiders are looking for when they watch your life?*

- *Give practical examples of how we can 'be wise to outsiders' (v5).*

Make the most of every opportunity

If we are going to be witnesses for Christ, we must take every opportunity. 'Be wise in the way you act towards outsiders; make the most of every opportunity' (v5). Paul is telling us to bargain hunt, snap up the opportunities we have. Christians live between two worlds, the world of the Bible and the world in which God has placed us. Here is an encouragement to work out what are those opportunities. There are natural opportunities that come up in national life, headlines and stories that grab people's attention.

Think of the recent tragic death of Stephen Oake, a Manchester detective killed whilst arresting a suspected terrorist. How amazingly well his family, Christians like him, spoke up for Jesus. There are personal circumstances that arise for us to bring God's focus, the gospel – a new baby, a birthday, a wedding, a funeral.

Eddie Lyle once coined a great phrase. He said, 'Too many Christians have been cagouled.' You grasp the picture especially if you come to the Lake District. People are togged up for that mountain walk. They can pull a cagoule over them and then they can just about see in front of themselves. Many of us are going through the world as cagouled Christians. We can just see a little bit in front of ourselves. But effectively we are blinkered. But we don't need 'cagouled' Christians! We need men and women with vision to see and understand the times and opportunities which the days we live in afford. We need a generation like those of the tribe of Issachar, who 'understood the times and knew what the people of God should do' (1 Chr. 12:32).

- *Often it is only with hindsight that we see there was an opportunity to share the gospel in a certain situation. Discuss what measures we can take to become more aware and ready to take gospel opportunities.*

- *Imagine yourself in conversation with a non-Christian friend and the following topics come up. Think of as many ways as possible to use these topics to introduce the gospel:*

  - *The events of September 11th, 2001*
  - *They announce they are having a baby*
  - *You see a poster advertising* Alpha *or* Christianity Explored

Salt and light

Next, to be witnesses we need to speak appropriately. 'Let your conversation be always full of grace, seasoned with salt' (v6). Be sensitive as you share the gospel, be gracious. There was a period in church history when hellfire and damnation preaching was particularly popular. What many people objected to was not so much the fact of judgement or hellfire and damnation, but the way some preachers seemed to delight fiendishly in dangling sinners over the fires of hell. There often seemed little graciousness. Robert Murray M'Cheyne was a nineteenth century Scottish minister in Dundee. He died before his thirtieth birthday in 1843. He was noted for his outstanding godliness and Christlikeness. Speaking to his friend, Andrew Bonar, one Monday morning he asked, 'Andrew, what did you preach on last night?' Bonar, a faithful minister of the gospel replied, 'I preached on hell.' M'Cheyne continued, 'Did the Lord enable you to preach it tenderly, my brother?'

> Tell me the story softly,
> With earnest tones and grave:
> Remember, I'm the sinner
> Whom Jesus came to save.
> Tell me that story always,
> If you would really be,
> In any time of trouble,
> A comforter to me.

Softly, tenderly – be winsome to win some!

● *How can we bring the comfort of the gospel to people, whilst at the same time presenting the whole picture of sin and hell?*

'Season your words with salt' – that is an interesting picture. In the ancient world, this phrase could mean using some wit as well as wisdom. The Jerusalem Bible translates it like this: 'Talk to them agreeably, and with a flavour of wit, and try to fit your answers to the needs of each one.' We need to try and work out where a person is and where they are coming from, what their real problems about faith are.

One day, I was doing some door-to-door evangelism, whilst I was a pastor in East London. I knocked at one door and a man appeared and asked, 'What do you want?' I said, 'I'm from the local church.' He replied, 'I'm not interested.' You can't do this with everyone but I said, 'What is it you're not interested in, because I haven't told you anything yet?' He looked at me for a moment and then said, 'I'm not interested in God.' So I replied, 'That's very interesting, because I think he's the most interesting person in the universe. How come you're not interested in him?' 'Easy,' he said, 'Because he doesn't exist.' I continued, 'Congratulations, you've got to have a lot of faith to be an atheist, haven't you?' Back came the reply, 'No, you haven't.' 'Of course you have, how can you prove there's no God?' 'Science,' he shot back. 'Which science proves there's no God?' 'Evolution!' End of the line? Not quite.

'Can I ask you another question?' I enquired, 'Are you into macro- or micro-evolution?' He looked puzzled: 'Look, pal, I'm having my dinner now. Could you come back tomorrow night?' I went back the next night and spoke to him for four hours about the God he didn't believe in. One thing we agreed on. The God he didn't believe in, I didn't believe in either, since such a God did not exist! Over a period of time, I was able to point him to the true and living God, and eventually he became a Christian. The point is that we cannot always 'content dump' on people. Use whatever wit and wisdom God has blessed you with. Listen as well as speak. Our aim isn't to win arguments but to communicate the gospel with a concern and a passion to see lost people come home to Jesus.

● *As verse 7 says, we need to be able to respond to people and their questions when we share the gospel. We are not all good at thinking on our feet, so is there any way we can prepare ourselves for these conversations? Discuss any practical ideas together.*

Remember there will be no evangelism in heaven. Too many evangelical churches are simply that – we are evangelical in doctrine but we've been neutered at our nerve level with regard to evangelism. If mission isn't at the heart of what we are about as churches, we have lost the plot. When we have, churches become ghettos, inward looking, and all sorts of problems arise. You have doubtlessly heard of the famous Pitcairn Island, Mutiny on the Bounty, Fletcher Christian and all that stuff. Do you know the island is in terminal decline? There are about three hundred people there now, and they are doomed to pass out of existence because their gene pool is too small. They are too in-bred. Unless hundreds of new people from outside move in, Pitcairn Island is doomed – that is just a sociological and biological fact.

Churches can get to that point too. There may be seventy or a hundred members at the church, but they are too in-bred because evangelism crept off the agenda a long time ago. No one has been converted in a long time. The church is now consumed by its maintenance rather than its mission. We have to encourage each other and our leaderships to stop merely looking within our churches, analysing and psycho-analysing our problems and felt needs. 'Open your eyes and look out to the fields! They are ripe for harvest', challenges Jesus (Jn. 4:35). Let's get our eyes on the harvest fields of our communities, of our countries and the nations of the world. It is a matter of perspective really. When you realise that the people you are speaking to for Christ have some massive problems – like their eternal destiny – those little problems you had about the flower rota – or the kind of music you use in the church – turn out to be not the big issues after all!

● *Analyse how your church is doing in evangelism. Think about:*

  ● *Your personal witness*
  ● *The effectiveness of your evangelistic services and special events*

● *Are there any lessons you can learn?*

Reflection and response

As individuals, make a list of five people whom you meet on a regular basis. Commit to praying for them and asking God to give you opportunities to share the gospel with them. As a group, think about doing an evangelistic event for your friends — a barbecue, a Christmas evening at someone's home with mince pies and carols, the possibilities are endless!

Chapter 15 – Pressing on

Aim: To keep going in Christian service

Focus on the theme

Think of a specific time when your passion to serve God was renewed. What gave you that renewed enthusiasm and determination to keep going? As you share your experiences, discuss the features they have in common.

Read: Colossians 4:2-18
Key verses: Colossians 4:7-18

Lone Rangers or team players?

Some people think of the apostle Paul as a Lone Ranger, a Clint Eastwood or Dirty Harry kind of figure, who bends the rules and cannot work with anybody. But actually in Paul's letters and the book of Acts, there are over a hundred different Christians mentioned with whom he had contact – he was a team player! In contrast, too many Christians want to be solo flyers. I have often heard people talking about one man ministry, where someone is paid to do all the church donkeywork. Somebody came to see me at my last church and said, 'I'm going to a church which meets my needs.' I replied, 'Well that's good. God bless you there.' But he wanted to make his point: 'No, no, I need to tell you why. In services in this church, you lead an occasional hymn but mainly you just preach and that's it. We then have all these other people leading worship, taking the children's talk and doing all sorts of things. So I am going to a church where the minister leads the service, reads the Bible, prays, does the children's talk and then preaches. He does everything.' Where in the Bible do we read that we should try and make one person indispensable? Do you know that piece entitled *The Indispensable Man*?

Sometimes when you are feeling important,
Sometimes when your ego's in bloom,
Sometimes when you take it for granted,
You're the best qualified in the room:
Sometimes when you feel that your going
Would leave an unfillable hole;
Just follow these simple instructions
And see how they humble your soul.
Take a bucket and fill it with water,
Put your hand in it up to the wrist,
Take it out, and the hole that remains
Is a measure of how much you'll be missed.
You can splash all you like when you enter,
You can stir up the water galore,
But stop! And you'll find that in no time,
It looks just the same as before.
The moral in this quaint example
Is to do just the best that you can;
Be proud of yourself but remember
There's no indispensable man!

Or indeed woman!

● *Paul knew he needed others, that others had a ministry to perform for God. So in these verses we learn some key principles about Christian service. On a scale of 1-10 1 being not very important and 10 very important) how would you rate the*

importance of church community in helping you persevere in your
Christian life?

God can use all sorts

Firstly, God uses all different types of people (v7-9). Paul introduces us to Tychicus. We don't know much about Tychicus but, if we trace references to him, we find that he was regularly on the move, here and there for Paul. He was Paul's equivalent of email, his mobile phone! He was 'a dear brother, a faithful minister and fellow-servant in the Lord' (v7). He was ready to be a key messenger, for Paul writes, 'I am sending him for the express purpose that you may know about our circumstances and that he may encourage your hearts' (v8). No doubt he would report to the Colossian believers the impact the gospel was having on Caesar's household, as we have noted already from Philippians 1:12-14, 4:22.

Tychicus' travelling companion was Onesimus. He was a different case altogether. He had recently become a Christian and is described as 'our faithful and dear brother', rather than a faithful minister. Read Philemon and you will learn all about Onesimus, the fugitive, the runaway slave. He had run away from Philemon and ran into Paul and was converted. He is a brilliant little cameo of 'God incidences' that lead to faith in Christ. There was also Aristarchus – 'My fellow-prisoner' (v10). Why was he a fellow prisoner? Perhaps because he had been imprisoned with Paul for his faith. But a prisoner of some standing like Paul was allowed two slaves. It is possible, therefore, that Aristarchus and possibly Epaphras volunteered to be Paul's 'slaves.' Why? So they could be with their brother in prison. Now that type of fellowship goes a little beyond tea and biscuits after the service, doesn't it?

We are also introduced to 'Jesus who is called Justus' (v11). Jesus was a common name in the first century. This Justus is one of God's unsung heroes. There is nothing much we can say about this man. He is just mentioned in passing. But his inclusion is notable. Perhaps, like so many of us, he sought to flourish in the inconspicuous, in the daily round and common task. In contrast to him, we have the famous missionary doctor Luke (v14). He wrote both a gospel and the Book of Acts, and was one of Paul's travelling companions – see how he joins the action at Troas – 'we' he says (Acts 16:10). Then there is: 'Mark, the cousin of Barnabas' (v10). That name has quite a story behind it. For Mark was the one who failed at his first attempt at missionary service, managing to cause a major rift between Paul and Barnabas (Acts 13:13 and 15:36-40). Mark is now with Paul again – a reminder that since failure need never be final with God, it need not be with others.

Do you get the picture? Paul had the writers of two of the gospels and the book of Acts in prison with him! Between the three of them they produced over half the books in the New Testament! That is fascinating. You never know what may become of those with whom you sit in class or sit next to in your office. I sometimes wonder where some of our students from Moorlands will end up – and delightfully discover them making a difference and leading others to Christ in many places, years after leaving college. Never underestimate God's power to take ordinary people and make them effective for him. The Lord uses all sorts of people, delighting in their diversity in Christ. By grace, that includes unlikely candidates like you and me!

● *Which of these Christians do you identify with most? Explain your answer to the group.*

  ● *Tychicus – always on the move for God, driven by the needs of ministry*
  ● *Onesimus – a new Christian just at the beginning of his Christian service*
  ● *Justus – serving God in quiet, unobtrusive ways*

- *Mark — conscious of past failures and grateful God has given him a second chance at service*

● *It isn't always easy to work with different characters in Christian ministry. What lessons have you learnt from working with other Christians?*

Prayer warriors wanted

Secondly, we need to serve God fervently, with passion. Note how Paul describes Epaphras as 'one of you and a servant of Christ Jesus … He is always wrestling in prayer for you, that you may stand firm in all the will of God, mature and fully assured. I vouch for him that he is working hard for you and those at Laodicea and Hierapolis' (v12-13). Every Christian is called to pray. Clearly, however, this man had a ministry of prayer, of intercession.

A famous name from a previous Keswick generation was Leith Samuel, who has now passed on to his eternal reward. About thirty years ago, I was leading a beach mission in Hoylake, near my native Liverpool. I was asked to visit an old lady. It turned out to be a Mrs Samuel, Leith's mother. She was just a little bag of bones in a bed. I was warned beforehand, 'Make sure you've got time on your hands when you go to see her.' I asked why. 'All that woman does is pray.' That sounded exciting to me. I was shown into her room, briefly introduced, and then she said, 'So nice to meet you, brother. I haven't got much time today, so let's just pray.' And for the next forty-five minutes, we were at the throne of God as this woman interceded for others. Yes, we are all called to pray, but God may give some of us this special ministry of prayer, of being a real 'prayer warrior'. However, do notice that Epaphras was not just prayerful. He was busy for Christ as well: 'I vouch for him that he is working hard for you' (v13). He was a man of prayer and action. That can be a rare combination. Some pray and do not act. Other act and do not pray. For an examples of this rare combination, check out Nehemiah chapters 1-6.

Paul introduces us to another faithful servant of the gospel – 'Nympha and the church in her house' (v15), is the NIV translation. As you may know, there are various textual variants, as they are called, different manuscript copies. Don't panic about that. It ensures our New Testament is the best preserved book by far from the whole of the ancient world. At this point, some manuscripts read 'Nymphas, and the church in his house', whilst the NIV prefers 'her house'! Indeed another manuscript confuses us even further, for it says 'their' house. The probability is that was Nympha – a woman's house. It was unusual for a woman to be the head of a home; either she was single, divorced or widowed. But here is part of the genius of the ancient church. They were concerned to grow in Christ, via their house churches. We know that house church is a loaded phrase today. The fact is that the early church did not bother themselves too much about church buildings. The main thing was to get the gospel out, women as well as men being involved. As a group they were fervent in God's service, eager to get his message out.

You may know of the phenomenal growth of the church in China these last fifty years, a growth unprecedented in the history of the Christian church. Much of the evangelism has taken place through the unofficial house churches, and many of the most used and courageous evangelists have been the women. Here in the UK, too many churches are consumed by trivial issues. A single-minded passion for God to get the gospel out by men and women is the need of the hour.

- *What are the key things that sap your spiritual fervency?*
- *As mature Christians there is a temptation to think we have arrived spiritually, that there is nothing more for us to learn. How can we make sure we continue growing in:*
  - *Our personal devotion to God*

- *Our ministries*
- *Our passion for church life*

Finishing well

The third key lesson we learn from this passage is to finish well. The Demas mentioned here is in all probability the very one Paul refers to in his last letter, and who 'in love with this present world, has forsaken me' (2 Tim. 4:10). Demas is the guy who did not press on, who lost his way, and who did not finish well because he did not finish at all.

What a contrast to Archippus. Paul says, 'Tell Archippus: "See to it that you complete the work you have received in the Lord"' (v17). Have you received a work in the Lord? Have you completed it? Anyone can start a marathon. But the aim isn't to start but to finish it. So, the marathon of faith requires not only starters but 'stickers.' Check out some inspiration for running this race in Hebrews 12:1-3.

Many years ago, I remember being at a cross-roads in ministry. I took time out to walk and talk with God, taking along just my Greek New Testament, having decided to read through Colossians again. My question was, 'Lord, is it time for a change, a move on from this church?' And these words just leapt out of the page to me. 'Tell Archippus: "Fulfil the ministry you have received in the Lord".' It was like an arrow to my heart: 'Lord, have I fulfilled the ministry you called me to here in East London?' The reply seemed to be a clear 'No! There's more for you to do here. You have only just begun!' It would be at least five years before it was right to move. So I returned to my ministry with renewed vigour. There are times to lay down and finish what God's given you. Some of us are getting on in years, we are still doing things we have been doing for years. It may be right to continue. But God may say, 'I want you to stop doing that now. You have completed it. Leave it for somebody else to do.' Others of us need to know that we have to keep going where we are in that little church that sometimes breaks our hearts. God's word to us is: fulfil the ministry you have received in the Lord.

A ship was in the midst of a terrible storm. A lady on board was wild with fear. She was becoming uncontrollable, full of panic, and demanding that she be taken to see the captain. Eventually, a steward radioed through to the bridge and the captain told him to bring her up. As she entered the bridge, she screamed, 'Oh sir! Are we going to drown? Are we going to drown? Is the boat going to go down?' The captain, quickly assessing the situation, looked at her and said, 'Madam, be quiet and I'll tell you.' She calmed down a little and he continued, 'I'm going to tell you straight what the deal is here. If the sides fall off this ship, we are going to go *out*. If the bottom drops off, we are going to go *down*. If the engine blows, Madam, I can tell you we are going to go *up*. But meanwhile, I intend to go *on*.'

Christians are to be people who intend to go on. Liverpool Football Club's fans at Anfield regularly sing (another pain for an Evertonian to admit) about walking through a storm holding your head up high and not being afraid of the dark. Why? Because larks and everything else will eventually sing? No. For the Christian, it is more solid than that. It is because Christ is at the end of the storm and, amazingly, Christ is with us in the storm. 'When you pass through the waters, I will be with you; and when you pass through the rivers, they will not sweep over you' (Is. 43:2). David Livingstone, the great missionary-explorer, prayed:

> Lord send me anywhere – only go with me;
> Lay any burden on me – only sustain me;
> Sever any tie, but the tie that binds me to Thyself.

It can be too soon to quit. Jesus did not. He completed the work his Father gave him to do (Jn. 17:4), the work of salvation.

As part of his church, do not quit what he has called you to do, till he tells you to do so. Do not lose your reward. Trust God and finish well. Christ is worth it! He is king of Heaven, Lord of Earth.

- *How do we know when it is time to move on from an area of service in the church? Brainstorm five possible tell-tale signs.*

- *In twos, talk about what work you feel the Lord has given you to complete — it could be a particular ministry, a family to raise, a country to pray for. Pray for each other that you may know the Lord's direction and guidance in this work.*

Further study

Find about more about Paul's associates. Read about Tychicus in Ephesians 6:21, Onesimus in Philemon, Aristarchus in Acts 19:29, 20:4, 27:2, Mark in Acts 15:38, 2 Timothy 4:11, Archippus in Philemon 2.

Reflection and response

Rather than dictating, Paul now takes the quill and writes the last section of the letter himself. The final prayer request he gave the Colossians was, 'Remember my chains' (v18). If you could give a final prayer request to your group, what would you want them to remember? Would you want them to pray for your non-Christian family members, a rebellious child, a difficult work situation? On a piece of paper, write down your own personal prayer request — 'Remember my...' and give it to another member of the group. Commit to praying for each other.

Review of Colossians 4:2-18

This last chapter of Colossians challenges us about our devotion to God in prayer, evangelism and in Christian service. We have been introduced to the team that worked with Paul — men who had failed God, those that were to give up and those that persevered in difficult times. Finishing strongly is a challenge to all of us. Think through the following questions to help you face this challenge:

- *What are the greatest temptations you face to give up on the Christian life?*
- *What are some of the lessons you wish an older Christian had taught you at the start of your Christian life?*
- *What are the strengths, gifts, interests that God has given you and you want to build on? How will you maximise them?*
- *What are your weaknesses and areas where you need the help of others? How will you make sure you have this help?*
- *What plans do you think God has for your life? Where do you think he is leading you and what steps are you taking to follow him?*

Points to Ponder

- *What have you learnt about God?*
- *What have you learnt about yourself?*
- *What actions or attitudes do you need to change as a result?*